Teaching Spelling

The Guide

Frances Mackay

Chapters

Published by
Hopscotch Educational Publishing Ltd
Unit 2, The Old Brushworks, 56 Pickwick Road,
Corsham, Wiltshire SN13 9BX
Tel: 01249 701701

© 2003 Hopscotch Educational Publishing

Written by Frances Mackay
Series design by Blade Communications
Cover design by Blade Communications
Illustrated by Bernard Connors
Printed by ?????????

ISBN 1-902239-81-4

Frances Mackay hereby asserts her moral right to
be identified as the author of this work in
accordance with the Copyright, Designs and Patents
Act, 1988.

ABOUT THIS RESOURCE

Teaching Spelling is a resource intended for use in primary and secondary schools to help teach children how to acquire the necessary knowledge, skills and confidence to become independent spellers.

The resource consists of two books:
The Guide
and
The Resource Book

The Guide

The Guide contains guidance for the teacher on how to teach spelling. It provides detailed background information on aspects of spelling such as: creating the right environment for teaching spelling; how to set up a spelling programme; ways to improve spelling; and spelling rules.

The Guide also contains a wealth of ideas and activities as well as extremely useful word lists. The activities can be 'dipped into' as and when required or integrated into any spelling programme the teacher may already be using.

The Resource Book

The Resource Book contains a huge collection of photocopiable activities that can be used in conjunction with *The Guide* but is designed to stand alone as a resource in itself.

The most practical feature of this book is the provision of differentiated activities. This enables the teacher to plan for group work for different ability levels. The differentiation can also be used to enable individuals to progress through a particular skill in stages or to provide additional challenges for homework.

ABOUT THIS BOOK

Teaching Spelling – The Guide aims to:
❑ support teachers by providing detailed background information and practical activities;
❑ provide useful word lists to save teachers time compiling their own;
❑ provide teachers with the confidence needed to teach spelling across a wide age and/or ability range;
❑ provide teachers with stimulating spelling activities that will encourage children to develop enjoyment and curiosity as well as knowledge and understanding.

The Guide is intended to be a reference book – to be 'dipped into' as and when required. However, it would be very beneficial to read Chapters 1 and 2 first because these chapters provide suggestions for good practice in the teaching of spelling and explain how teachers can create the right classroom atmosphere to enable children to build a confident approach to spelling.

Within each chapter there are numerous spelling activity suggestions that relate to the content of the chapter. These are intended to provide the teacher with ideas that can be easily introduced into the classroom as simple games and puzzles to solve. The activities can be adapted to different age/ability levels and can easily form part of any current spelling programme the teacher may already use.

The photocopiable activities in *The Resource Book* also relate to each chapter of *The Guide*. In Chapter 2, for example, *The Guide* explains the term 'mnemonics' and then provides the teacher with lots of examples of the different types of mnemonics, such as grouping words that go together, acronyms, rhymes and chants, identifying difficult letter combinations and using word families. The teacher can use the ideas on these pages to introduce or revise mnemonics with the children and then provide them with follow-up differentiated photocopiable activities from *The Resource Book*.

Learning to spell in the English language is not an easy task for any of us! We hope that the ideas contained in this resource will enable teachers to make the teaching and learning of spelling a fun as well as a purposeful experience. We also hope that the useful hints and 'tricks' suggested will provide the children with useful tools that they can continue to use throughout their lives, thereby making them more confident spellers.

Teaching spelling

Creating the right environment

In essence, spelling is both 'caught' and 'taught'! Children learn to spell best in a literacy-rich environment where they are encouraged to explore and have fun with words and to share their writing and reading with others. They should 'take risks' with their writing as this helps to promote a natural curiosity about our language that enables them to feel confident enough to 'have a go' at reading and writing words that are unfamiliar. But the mastery of spelling skills cannot be acquired merely by exposure to words alone – children also need a complementary structured approach that takes into account their stage of development in literacy skills and understanding.

Children need a mixture of support, encouragement and challenge to ensure that they gain the confidence needed to move forward in their spelling development. Teachers who understand where children are in this development will be able to provide the explicit teaching necessary to move them forward. (Refer to page 6 for details of the stages of development.)

What makes a classroom conducive to acquiring spelling skills? In a literacy-rich classroom, the walls are filled with print resources with which the children can interact, the classroom library is well organised and contains a wealth of exciting books on display and there are reference resources that enable them to develop their skills as independent learners. Specifically, the classroom may contain:

1 WORD WALLS

A word wall is an area of the classroom that is devoted to the display and study of words. The wall is designed to be used by all the children and helps to promote group learning. The wall consists of lists of words arranged alphabetically and may include library pockets where the words are written separately on pieces of card.

The word wall should be dynamic and changing – not a static display that remains unchanged for a whole term! The words on the wall could include:

❏ words the children use in their writing and have difficulty spelling
❏ words that relate to the class topic
❏ words with particular beginnings
❏ homophones
❏ contractions
❏ compound words
❏ the children's names
❏ high frequency words

Word walls are most effective when the teacher calls attention to each new word and helps the children understand how that word can be used and how they might remember how to spell it (using techniques such as mnemonics). But more importantly, perhaps, it needs to be the children's word wall. The children should be encouraged to make decisions about which words to put on the wall (and which words to remove).

The wall can be used in a variety of ways:

❏ to reinforce alphabetical order
❏ to play games with
❏ to act as a reference when writing
❏ to reinforce particular spelling patterns or rules
❏ to encourage the discussion, exploration and enjoyment of words
❏ to develop group sharing and learning

2 LABELS

Labels can be very effective tools for literacy learning, especially when they have been chosen and written co-operatively between the teacher and the children. Labels can be used in the following ways:

❏ to indicate where classroom items belong
❏ to provide instructions on how to use classroom items
❏ to stimulate interactive responses to classroom displays
❏ to organise classroom resources such as the class library
❏ to act as word banks

As with the word wall, labels need to be dynamic and interactive. The teacher needs to repeatedly draw the children's attention to the words on the labels in different ways – by using the words in games, by using the words as examples when reinforcing a spelling pattern or rule and by encouraging the children to use the words as a reference source in their reading and writing.

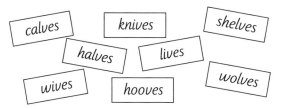

3 WORD CHARTS

Charts can be very useful learning tools for literacy, both when they are being created (such as in a shared or guided writing activity using a flip-chart) and when they are put up on display. Charts that relate to spelling can include:

- words in a particular spelling family
- palindromes
- words with specific letter sounds
- words grouped into number of syllables
- compound words
- silent letter words
- words that rhyme
- double letter words
- plurals
- tricky spellings

As with word walls and labels, the word charts work best if they are used in an interactive way as part of everyday lessons – to avoid them becoming just decorative wallpaper!

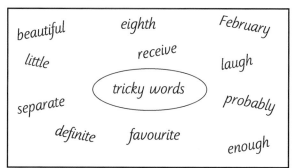

4 REFERENCE RESOURCES AREA

A literacy-rich classroom will have an abundance of resources available that will encourage the children to become independent learners. It is the teacher's role to teach the children the value of these resources and this includes *when* as well as *how* to use them. A child who constantly looks up words in a dictionary as she writes, for example, will not develop the expertise and confidence of a writer who has learned to check and edit her work *after* it has been written.

Reference resources may include:

- internet access
- dictionaries – different kinds, to include picture, school and rhyming dictionaries
- thesauruses
- glossaries
- word play books such as riddles
- encyclopaedias
- word books made by the children

A classroom environment that encourages children to get into the habit of referring to such references without being directed will help the children to become competent 'problem solvers' enabling them to become increasingly independent.

5 WRITING AREA

Having a special area set aside to assist the children in their writing encourages them to explore and experiment with making words. This area can include magnetic letters, letter and word tiles and materials for making letters in classes for younger children, as well as stamps, special writing paper and pens, alphabet charts, handwriting resources and word games.

Developmental stages in spelling

The following chart outlines the developmental stages in spelling and the teacher's role in helping the child to progress through the stages.

Stage	Teaching and learning activities
Beginning – the child: is becoming aware of the sounds in words and some visual features of print; experiments with making marks on paper; recognises own name (or part of it) in print.	**Beginning – the teacher:** provides models of correctly written words in response to the child's writing; uses rhymes, songs, repetitions and chants; uses shared reading and writing; uses lots of activities involving children's names and the alphabet; draws attention to the relationship between sounds and letters; uses alphabet frieze; teaches pencil grip.
Emergent – the child: understands that words are made up of sounds and can connect some sounds with letters (usually consonants); can recognise a few high frequency words; recognises own name and can write part of it; uses letter names to represent some sounds in writing; represents a whole word with one, two or three letters.	**Emergent – the teacher:** continues work with the alphabet; teaches children to segment words into syllables; uses onset and rime games and activities; helps children represent sounds heard in words with letters written in the order they are heard; models the use of class spelling charts; teaches children to use word banks and personal dictionaries; helps children to understand starting points and direction when forming letters.
Early – the child: knows many sound-letter/letter-cluster relationships and patterns; hears and writes consonant and dominant vowel sounds in words; knows the names of the letters of the alphabet and related sounds; has a sense of a sentence; develops particular spellings for certain sounds using self-formulated rules, such as 'wos' (was).	**Early – the teacher:** teaches a range of word identification strategies, such as identifying little words in big words; explores common letter sequences, visual patterns, word components, sounding out; teaches some word learning strategies, such as *Look, Say, Cover, Write, Check*; explores connections between words and regular spelling patterns; teaches children to identify letters representing different sounds and sounds represented by different letters; fosters clear and fluent handwriting; links handwriting to spelling.
Transitional – the child: knows consonant and vowel patterns and relationships between letters, letter clusters and sounds; uses this information to construct words in writing; hears most sounds; indicates in spelling that there is a sound in each syllable; is aware of the importance and quality of handwriting.	**Transitional – the teacher:** introduces other word identification strategies, such as blending, sight words, segmentation, root words, prefixes, suffixes; continues to teach visual patterns; explores spelling rules; uses mnemonics; encourages children to experiment with a range of scripts and to take pride in their handwriting.
Conventional – the child: understands the variety of rules and principles of how words work; knows when a word is spelled wrongly and is able to rectify the mistake; can use historical roots to derive meaning; uses inflections, plurals and affixes correctly; writes fluently; is becoming a competent and independent writer.	**Conventional – the teacher:** focuses on meaning as a guide to spelling; teaches complex patterns and irregular spellings; develops memory aids; extends knowledge of affixes; fosters development of a fluent, individual handwriting style that can be adapted to suit different purposes.

Spelling activities – beginning stage

1 Play games using the children's names. Can they make up rhyming couplets for names? For example:

> Here comes Paul;
> He is very tall.
> or
> Lynita likes to draw;
> There's her picture on the door!

2 Play I-spy, using the beginning sounds of objects in the room.

3 Go on letter hunts! Ask the children to find words in magazines and newspapers that begin with a particular letter. They could cut the words out for a class dictionary.

4 Ask the children to sort their name cards in different ways:
- ❏ by length – long names and short names
- ❏ by initial letter
- ❏ in alphabetical order

Spelling activities – emergent stage

1 Have fun making up alliterative rhymes using the children's names.

2 Play 'Find the sound'. Ask the children to find a particular initial or final phoneme in shared reading activities. How many words can they find with this sound? The teacher can model writing sentences using these words.

3 Make up some cards with a picture and its word. Make sure there are words that rhyme. The children can play games where they sort the words into sets that rhyme, or play rhyme snap.

4 Play 'Guess the name'. Write the initial letter of a child's name followed by dashes for each letter. For example:

> F _ _ _ _ _

Can they tell by the length of the word? What letter could come second? Establish that letters such as 'z', 'w' and 'b' would be very unlikely. Extend this activity to other words, encouraging the children to suggest the most likely letters – not just guess.

Spelling activities – early stage

1 Using words on card, play sorting games. The teacher could sort the words (for example, according to number of syllables) and the children have to guess how they have been sorted. The children could sort them according to their own criteria also.

2 Make up cloze activities where all the answers have the same sound or same visual pattern.

3 Challenge the children to create new words by removing one letter of a word and replacing it with a new one. For example:
pin – pan; fan – fat; cat – cot; cod – pod

4 Challenge the children to find little words in big words.

5 Carry out onset and rime activities. Ask the children to list all the letters that could go in front of a word ending to make a list of words. For example, how many words can you make that end in 'ent'?

6 Ask the children to make up rhymes using alliteration.

7 Play 'Rhyming pairs'. Write words that rhyme on cards. Spread the cards out face down. The children take it in turns to turn over two cards. If they are a rhyming pair, they keep the cards. If not, the cards are returned to their place.

8 Ask the children to choose ten words from their own spelling list. They write the words on cards and sort them in different ways:
- ❏ words with the same initial or final sound
- ❏ words with the same number of syllables
- ❏ alphabetical order
- ❏ words of the same length
- ❏ words with the same letter pattern
- ❏ words with double letters

Challenge them to make up mnemonics to help them remember how to spell these words.

Spelling activities – transitional stage

1 Play word sorting games where the children have to sort the words according to their own criteria and ask a partner to work out how they have been sorted. Words could be sorted according to the number of syllables, compound and non-compound words, common letter strings, plural and singular and so on.

2 Play card games with word cards. The children could play snap or rummy where the pairs have to be matched according to an agreed criterion, such as number of syllables.

3 Challenge the children to use their own spelling word lists (or personal dictionaries) to create puzzles with the words. Can they link them together in some way – in a step, square, wavy or snake pattern?

```
garden
     i
     n
     e
     t
  young
       r
       e
       a
       tired
```

4 Play word games such as 'Add a letter'. Give the children words plus an additional letter. Can they make a new word? For example: tar + s = star
eve + n = even
mad + i = maid

This can be extended to adding further letters:
eve + n + s = seven

5 Play 'New words'. Give the children words where they have to rearrange the letters to form new words. For example:
nest – tens
lose – sole
thorn – north
wrong – grown

6 Challenge the children to write a sentence using the letters of a given word. Use dictionaries. For example:

horse
Harry ordered red socks eventually.

This is a form of mnemonics and can help children remember how to spell tricky words.

Spelling activities – conventional stage

1 Challenge the children to make up their own crossword puzzles, using a dictionary to help them with the clues.

2 Play 'Create a word'. Write each consonant on a piece of paper and put them into a container. Write five of each vowel on pieces of paper and put them into a different container. Ask the children to draw the following grid:

w	b	l	e	be	web	we	blew

Ask four different children to pick out three consonants and one vowel each. As the letters are called out, each child writes the letters in the squares and then uses the letters to make up a word or words. This activity could be timed so they have to race to create the word(s). Score four points for each four-letter word created, three points for a three-letter word, two points for a two-letter word and one point for a one-letter word. Dictionaries could be allowed. This game could also be played in teams.

3 Provide the children with a 5 x 5 grid. Call out letters at random. Each child decides where to place each letter on their grid. The aim of the game is to strategically place the letters to make words. The words can be horizontal, vertical or diagonal. The person with the most words wins or the words could be scored; for example, five points for a five-letter word, four points for a four-letter word and so on.

t	e			
	m	a	n	
			o	
w				s

Organising a spelling programme

Every school should have a spelling policy which outlines the methodologies to be used and the organisation and management of the subject within the school. It is usually up to each teacher to then prepare their own spelling programme within the guidelines of this policy. What follows here are some suggestions for how this programme might be organised.

Good spellers learn how to spell a large number of words because they have learned strategies that allow them to use a problem-solving approach to unfamiliar words. They have internalised the basic spelling patterns, rules and principles that enable them to approach the spelling of new words from a confident, analytical starting point. Teaching that emphasises this problem-solving approach to spelling is far more effective than teaching that only requires the children to memorise lists of words.

Spelling lists, however, are very important. But it is how these lists are compiled and how the children are encouraged to learn the words that are crucial to the success of the spelling programme.

COMPILING SPELLING LISTS

It is important that the children's spelling lists are individualised as much as possible. Ideally, the list should contain:

1   words that the children have misspelled in their own writing
2   words that the children need to use in the context of the curriculum
3   words that relate to specific spelling patterns or rules

One way for the teacher to keep a record of the children's own spelling errors is to keep a file or book with a designated page for each child. The teacher can then write any errors in this book during the course of the day from the children's writing in any subject area.

The number of words to be learned each week needs careful consideration. It can be very daunting for less confident spellers to have to learn 20 new words every week (and fail miserably in a spelling test week after week!). This will only help to convince them even further of their inadequacies and will turn them off trying to improve their spelling even more! Much better for these children to give them two to five words to learn each day so that they are more assured of success.

It is also a good idea to involve the children in compiling the lists. The teacher can choose some words (that relate to the class topic or spelling pattern being addressed) and the children can choose others (selected from errors they have made in their own writing or words they want to use but do not know how to spell).

HOW TO LEARN THE WORDS

Time needs to be set aside (say 5 to 15 minutes) each day for learning the words. The children could have a spelling journal in which to do this. The words need to be copied accurately from an agreed source (either the teacher or the child can do this) and the list needs to be checked before the child begins to learn the words.

The children then learn the words using a variety of strategies (such as 'Look, say, cover, write, check', mnemonics and looking for little words in big words).

The children could then work in pairs to check their progress. One child could read out the words while the other writes them. The lists could then be handed in to the teacher to check. After two or three correct spellings the words can be ticked off the child's list (in the teacher's spelling book). Words that are incorrect need to be considered again – perhaps there is a better way for the child to remember how to spell these words. Their spelling partner may come up with ideas to help! It is often helpful to learn problem words by learning them together with other words that follow a similar pattern – learning by analogy can be very effective.

OTHER ASPECTS OF THE SPELLING PROGRAMME

Alongside the learning of individual spelling lists, there also need to be whole class teaching sessions and follow-up group work where the children are able to work at their own level.

Schools also need to decide whether or not to include spelling within the school's homework programme. Teachers need to take great care in briefing parents on how to help their child with spelling. Too much home pressure can create problems, but carefully thought out homework activities can be extremely beneficial. Parents need to be made aware of the ways they can give positive support to their children. Some schools prepare parent booklets with guidelines for helping with reading and writing and/or hold special parents' evenings.

Assessment

There are several different ways to assess children's spelling progress. Here are some of them:

1 OBSERVATION

The teacher can observe the following:
- ❑ What does the child do when she doesn't know how to spell a word?
- ❑ Is the child willing to take risks and 'have a go'?
- ❑ Does the child notice errors in her own work? Is she willing to make corrections?
- ❑ Does the child show an interest in words?
- ❑ How well does the child use spelling resources?
- ❑ What evidence is there of the child's understanding of letter/sound relationships?
- ❑ What strategies does the child use to learn new words?
- ❑ What strategies does the child use to spell unfamiliar words?

Such observations can take place during shared and guided reading and writing sessions as well as during independent writing. It is also helpful to conduct short interviews or conferences with each child, especially with older children. You can prepare some simple questions beforehand, such as 'What do you do when you come across a word you do not know?', 'What do you do to help you remember how to spell a word?', 'Do you have any words that you find tricky to spell?', 'Do you think it is important to learn how to spell words correctly?' and 'How do you think you might be able to improve your spelling?'

2 WORK SAMPLES

Keeping a portfolio of work samples is an excellent way of recording children's progress. The work needs to be chosen at predetermined times for each child so that progress can be measured methodically. The samples need to be annotated. It is the analysis of the work that is important – we need to understand what kinds of mistakes the child is making in order to set meaningful future learning targets.

3 SELF-ASSESSMENT

It is very worthwhile to involve the children in their own spelling development. They can keep spelling journals or logbooks in which they record any problems or successes they have had with spelling that week. They could also complete a 'What I can do' sheet at the end of each term so that they can see for themselves where they need help next. (See the example below.)

Name_____ Date_____		
Things I know and can do in spelling	☹	☺
I am very good at 'having a go'. I can divide words into syllables. I can change words into the plural. I am beginning to learn when to double letters; for example, hop, hopped. I can use 'Look, say, cover, write, check' to learn words. I enjoy learning about words. I can use a dictionary to look up a word. I can check my work to look for mistakes. I know what to do if I don't know how to spell a word. I know about silent letters in words. I know what a compound word is. I know what a suffix is. I know what a prefix is. I know what a homophone is. I can put words into alphabetical order. I know some spelling rules.		

4 FORMAL ASSESSMENT

Occasionally, the teacher may see a need to carry out a more formal assessment. There are various diagnostic and standardised tests available that may help determine spelling targets for individual children. Tests include:

British Spelling Test series (BSTS 1–5) by D Vincent and M Crumpler, NFER-NELSON
Young's Parallel Spelling (6–15 years), Hodder and Stoughton
Vernon Graded Word Spelling Test (6–17.6 years), Hodder and Stoughton
Parallel Spelling Tests (Year 2 – Year 7), Hodder and Stoughton
SPAR (Spelling and Reading) Tests (Year 3 or older children with a reading age of up to 9 years), Hodder and Stoughton

Chapter 2

Ways to improve spelling

Building confidence

Some people seem to be naturally good spellers while others find it a constant struggle. Sometimes this struggle can be due to specific learning difficulties and sometimes it can be due to a reluctance to 'have a go' for fear of failing. Whatever the reason, struggling spellers often become reluctant writers and the less they write, the less able they are to practise the skills of spelling and so the cycle of poor spelling and poor self image continues.

The key to breaking out of this cycle is to develop confidence in approaching spelling. The more practice a writer has and the more willing he/she is to 'have a go', the more accurate their spelling will become. Children need to view themselves as 'apprentice' writers – constantly developing and changing over a lifetime. They need to be made aware that everyone, even the very best of authors, can and does make mistakes, and that everyone can find ways to improve their spelling. They also need to be made aware that English can be a very difficult language to learn and that spelling, in particular, can be extremely tricky because words don't always conform to a certain pattern or rule!

What do 'good' spellers do?

What techniques do good spellers use that help them with spelling?

1   If they are unsure of a spelling, they write the word several different ways to see which one 'looks right'. Spelling is a visual skill.

2   They say the word to themselves to see how it sounds.

3   They visualise the word in their mind.

4   They break words into syllables.

5   They think about what is the most likely way to spell the word – they associate it with similar words they already know.

6   They think of words that have a similar spelling pattern; for example, 'house', 'mouse'.

7   They say the word in a special way to help them remember how to spell it; for example, 'Wed – nes – day'.

8   They look for little words in bigger words; for example, 'govern' + 'me' (government).

	Ways to build confidence in spelling
1	Believe that you CAN improve your spelling – don't see yourself as being hopeless.
2	'Have a go' at spelling unfamiliar words – don't rely on a dictionary too much.
3	Write in a joined-up style, instead of printing. A fluent handwriting style aids spelling.
4	Check through your work carefully when you have finished it. Read it to see if it makes sense. Underline any words you think are incorrect, rather than relying on others, such as a teacher, to check for you. This helps you to develop an 'eye' for spelling.
5	Take an interest in words. Have fun finding unusual words. Try to learn some difficult ones to impress others!
6	Make a point of learning those words you often get incorrect. Make up a rhyme or phrase to help you with the trickiest ones (mnemonic); for example: A **pie**ce of **pie**.

How to develop visual memory

Spelling is a visual skill. Good spellers know a word is correct because it 'looks right'. It is this visual memory that is the key to confident spelling.

1 PLAY VISUAL MEMORY GAMES

a   Play the age-old memory game where a selection of everyday objects is placed on a tray. Players are given a time limit before the tray is taken away. How many of the objects can they remember? The idea is to try and visualise each item as it was on the tray.

b   Play detectives in a game called 'What's changed?' Ask a child to stand in a pose like a statue. Everyone else tries to memorise everything about the person – the pose and their clothing. Everyone turns around and the teacher changes ONE thing about the pose; for example, undoes a shoelace, turns down a collar or puts a plait behind rather than in front. The others turn back and work out what has been changed.

Such simple games help to train visual memory and can also be applied to spelling activities. Encourage the children to play memory card games – the pack could contain pairs with the same letter pattern or pairs of the same words. The children shuffle the cards and place them face down. They take turns to turn over two cards – if they match they keep them – if not, they are returned face down. Can they remember where a card is to make a match?

The teacher can also help develop visual memory skills when the children ask for a spelling. The teacher can write it down on a piece of paper, ask the child to look at it and try to memorise it, and then ask them to carry it back to their desk 'in their head' and write it down as a whole word.

2 LOOK AT THE SHAPE OF WORDS

Words have distinctive shapes and noticing this can develop our visual memory of the words. For example:

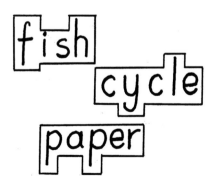

3 TRACE THE SHAPE OF WORDS

Sometimes tracing the shape of a word with a finger helps to 'implant' the visual shape of the word. Saying each part as it is traced also helps. Sometimes the words can be 'written' in a 3-D medium to aid this (for example, writing the words in glue and then sprinkling sand over them). A multi-sensory approach where words are written, spoken and traced can help children with specific learning difficulties.

4 USE A VISUAL MNEMONIC

A mnemonic is a way of helping us remember things. It can be a rhyme or a saying or it can be a visual memory jog; for example:

5 LEARN NEW WORDS USING A VISUAL TECHNIQUE

Use the 'Look, say, cover, write, check' method to learn new words.

The 'Look' part of this method is the most important part. Tell the children to visualise the word in their head. Look for words within words. Look for groups of letters that seem to go together. Concentrate on the tricky part of the word. Tell them to close their eyes and visualise the whole word. Explain that there should be no 'cheating' when they cover the word by peeping at it again! Tell them to say the word as they are writing it and then check very carefully to see if they are right.

The key is not to copy a word letter by letter but to memorise the whole word.

Play 'Spelling flash'. Write some words on separate pieces of card. Flash the cards to the children (the time limit can get progressively shorter). Ask them to memorise the whole word and write it down. How many do they get right? Score points according to visual clues; for example, for remembering the beginning letters, a spelling pattern such as 'tion', or a word within the word.

Look
Say
Cover
Write
Check

Spelling activities – developing visual memory

1 Play 'Which one is missing?' This game can be played in pairs, small groups or with the whole class. Six word cards are selected – they could relate to a specific spelling list or the class topic. The six cards are put on display. Everyone studies the cards and then closes their eyes. Someone removes one of the cards. Tell the others to open their eyes. Who can work out which word is missing? This game can be made more complicated by removing a word and then mixing up the order of the cards or by only flashing the cards initially and not leaving them on display.

| stair | chair | fair | lair | ? | hair |

2 Play 'Concentration'. Make up a set of word cards containing pairs of words. The players shuffle the cards and lay them out face down. Each player takes it in turns to turn over two cards – if they match they keep them – if not, they are returned to their place face down. Can the children visualise where the words are? The game continues until all the words are matched.

who			
			who

3 Write some words on cards. They could relate to the children's own spelling lists or be a set of tricky words. Place them face up. Ask the children to look at the words for a set time. Then cover the words. How many of them can they remember? They could say or write the words. This game can be made easier or more difficult by altering the number and familiarity of the words.

came	face	game
make	late	ate
tale	gave	same

4 Prepare some word searches containing words with the same letter patterns or spelling rule.

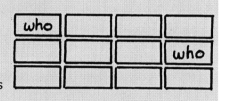

find these words…
bridge
edge
lodge
fridge
judge

f	t	w	r	b	s	o
r	b	t	o	r	s	w
i	r	a	e	i	t	e
d	b	z	i	d	d	a
g	l	o	d	g	e	j
e	a	w	e	e	m	v
n	d	p	s	f	y	d
p	g	w	e	n	d	g
t	e	r	s	t	w	e

5 Play 'Spot the correct word'. Write out groups of words where only one spelling is correct in each set. How quickly can the children spot the correct one?

muther	because	lisen	among	littel
mother	becuse	lissen	amoung	little
motha	becorse	listen	amung	litle

6 Play 'Odd one out'. Write out a list of words where all the words except one have the same spelling pattern or rule. Can the children spot the odd one out?

mime	sink	stun
dime	think	nuts
time	thick	spun
grim	drink	fun

Mnemonics

A mnemonic is an aid to memory. It can be a rhyme, a saying, an acronym or any other device a person uses to help them remember things. The most useful mnemonics are usually those you make up yourself – but there are some very well-known ones.
For example:

Richard **o**f **Y**ork **g**ave **b**attle **i**n **v**ain
(The colours of the rainbow: red, orange, yellow, green, blue, indigo, violet)

30 days hath September,
April, June and November.
All the rest have 31
Excepting February alone
Which has 28 days clear,
And 29 each leap year.

Red sky at night, shepherd's delight.
Red sky in the morning, shepherd's warning.

Every **G**ood **B**oy **D**eserves **F**avour
(Music notes: E, G, B, D, F)

My **V**ery **E**asy **M**ethod: **J**ust **S**et **U**p **N**ine **P**lanets
(Mercury, Venus, Earth, Mars, Jupiter, Saturn, Uranus, Neptune, Pluto)

Mnemonics are very useful in helping us remember tricky spellings. Learning about the different types of mnemonics can give you ideas for developing some of your own:

1 GROUPING WORDS THAT GO TOGETHER

For example:

A p<u>ie</u>ce of p<u>ie</u>
You h<u>ear</u> with your <u>ears</u>
H<u>igh</u> and m<u>igh</u>ty
People go on a <u>bus</u> to <u>bus</u>iness
Never <u>end</u> a fri<u>end</u>ship
<u>Here</u>, t<u>here</u> and everyw<u>here</u>
We gr<u>eet</u> people we m<u>eet</u>
An <u>is</u>land <u>is</u> land
S<u>eat</u>s <u>eat</u> m<u>eat</u>
<u>Ice</u> is a noun and so is pract<u>ice</u>
A r<u>ui</u>ned s<u>ui</u>t
He can <u>eat</u> a gr<u>eat</u> d<u>eal</u>
Twins are d<u>ou</u>ble the tr<u>ou</u>ble
My <u>pal</u> is the princi<u>pal</u>
<u>Add</u> an <u>add</u>ress to your letter
The grocer sells mang<u>oes</u>, potat<u>oes</u> and tomat<u>oes</u>
A princi<u>ple</u> is a ru<u>le</u>
Be w<u>ise</u>, comprom<u>ise</u>
I gr<u>asp</u> the r<u>asp</u>berry
A porp<u>oise</u> makes an interesting n<u>oise</u>

2 ACRONYMS

An acronym is a word made up from the initial letters of other words; for example: NATO (North Atlantic Treaty Organisation). If you have trouble remembering how to spell a particular word, it can be helpful to treat it as an acronym and find a word for each letter of the tricky word. This is a very widely used form of mnemonics – and often it is the silliest ones that you remember best!

For example:

big **e**lephants **c**annot **a**lways **u**se **s**mall **e**scalators = b e c a u s e

General **E**isenhower's **o**ldest **g**irl **r**ode **a** **p**ony **h**ome **y**esterday = g e o g r a p h y

not **e**very **c**at **e**ats **s**ardines, **s**hrimps **and** **r**abbit **y**oghurt = n e c e s s a r y

cats **a**re **u**sually **g**ood **h**amster **t**ormentors = c a u g h t

orange **u**nderwear – **r**eally! = o u r

every **n**ew **e**lf **m**ust **y**ell = e n e m y

giant **r**abbits **a**re **p**retty **h**opeless **s**ailors = g r a p h s

some **p**eople **e**at **c**akes **i**n **a** **l**ay-by = s p e c i a l

she **i**s **g**oing **h**ome = s i g h

little **a**pes **s**it **a**nd **g**obble **n**uts **e**nergetically = l a s a g n e

ghosts **h**ate **o**ther **s**pooky **t**ypes = g h o s t

a **n**ew **y**ear = a n y

we **a**re **t**errible **e**aters **r**eally = w a t e r

fish **e**njoy **b**umping **r**ound **u**nder **a**ny **r**acing **y**achts = F e b r u a r y

3 RHYMES AND CHANTS

Making up a rhyme or chant can be a very useful way of remembering difficult spellings. Sometimes, just saying the letters out loud to yourself can help.

For example:

M - i - ss - i - ss - i - pp - i

(say: m, i, double s, i, double s, i, double p, i)

or   on – i – on
        mur – mur
        ba – na – na
        in – ter – ested
        bound – a – ries
        gov – ern – ment
        can – di – date
        q – ue – ue
        min – i – mum

Further examples:

Use 'i' before 'e',
Except after 'c'.
When 'a' or 'i' is the sound,
It's the other way round.

Practice with a 'c' a noun can only be.
Practise with an 's' is just a verb, I guess.

cemetery – we get there with ease (e's)

The wicked bandit
Who practised dec**ei**t
Gazed at the c**ei**ling
And s**ei**zed the rec**ei**pt

4 IDENTIFYING DIFFICULT LETTER COMBINATIONS

Sometimes it helps to remember a spelling by concentrating on just the difficult letter combinations in the word.

For example:

ne**cess**ary = **one c**ollar and **two s**ocks
profe**ss**or = **one f**rog and **two s**nakes
a**wkw**ard = **W**illiam **K W**illiam
emba**rr**a**ss**ed = **two r**ed cheeks and **two s**carlet ears
the **CID** investigates a**ccid**ents and in**cid**ents
a**cc**o**mm**odation = a – **cc** – o – **mm** – o
beau**t**iful = **b**ig elephants **a**ren't **u**gly
two 'm's, two 't's and **two 'e's** in co**mmittee**
o**cc**a**s**ion = **two c**ollars and **one s**ock
there's **a rat** in sep**ara**te

5 WORD FAMILIES

Learning words in families where the words have the same spelling pattern improves spelling by developing visual memory skills.

For example:

arrow	reign	vague
barrow	weigh	league
narrow	neighbour	fatigue
yellow	sleigh	guest

shop	village	name
shopped	voyage	blame
shopping	message	same
shopper	cottage	game

Spelling activities – mnemonics

1 Play 'Happy families' where the cards that have to be matched are words that belong to the same spelling family.

2 Play 'Acronym challenge'. Challenge the children to think of as many different acronyms as they can for a particular word; for example, 'our':
    open up, Roger!
    orange underwear – really!
    ostriches upset rangers
    officers untie robber

3 Ask the children to ask their parents for any mnemonics they know – build up a class collection and put it on display.

4 Have fun making difficult words look like their meaning; for example:

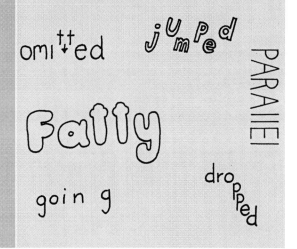

Syllables

A syllable is a word or part of a word which is pronounced as a unit. Each syllable contains a single vowel sound (sometimes 'y' makes a vowel sound – as in 'marry').

Words can be:
- monosyllabic (one syllable, such as 'pen')
- disyllabic (two syllables, such as 'pencil')
- polysyllabic (three or more syllables, such as 'pendulum')

When trying to spell a longer word it can be very helpful to break it into syllables because this enables you to break the word into more manageable units. It helps you to look more closely at a word.

Some words are misspelled because a part of the word or a letter in it is difficult to hear. Saying each syllable of a word can help us to hear the part that is often left out; for example:

choc/**o**/late

in/**ter**/est/ing

sep/**ar**/ate

gen/**er**/al

THINGS TO REMEMBER ABOUT SYLLABLES

1 Every syllable has a vowel (or 'y') in it. A syllable can be a vowel on its own. For example, a/gain.

2 If double consonants appear in a word make the syllable division between the two letters. For example, kit/ten.

3 The division of syllables can be shown with a forward slash (/) or a dash (–). For example, mur/mur or mur – mur.

4 Endings and prefixes are usually syllables in themselves. For example, jump/ing, re/do.

HOW SYLLABIFICATION HELPS WITH SPELLING

Breaking words into syllables can help you with spelling in the following ways:

1 It makes the spelling of longer words easier by breaking them into smaller parts.

2 It helps you to realise how words are made up.

3 It forces you to look more carefully at the structure of words.

4 It helps you to see smaller words within longer words.

Unfortunately, there is a problem with dividing words into syllables to help with spelling. English is not a phonetically regular language. This means that when you sound out the separate syllables, you may find you have chosen the wrong combination of letters to represent the sound; for example:

fur/ni/ture

- 'fur' could be spelled 'fir' or 'fer'
- 'ni' could be 'ne'
- you may want to begin 'ture' with 'ch'

Syllabification, therefore, is a useful spelling technique only if used alongside other techniques and works best with words that are spelled as they sound, such as gar/den and pen/dant.

Spelling activities – syllables

1 Explore poetry forms, such as haiku, that use a syllable pattern.

2 Play rounds where each person in the circle has to say (and everyone clap) a word with one syllable until everyone has had a turn; then go around the circle again saying two-, then three-syllable words. Let the children 'pass' in order to keep the rhythm going.

3 Play 'Spelling cricket'. Two teams. One team 'bowls' by holding up a card with 1, 2, 3 or 4 on it. The other team 'bats' by saying a word with that number of syllables. Score 1 run for a one-syllable word, 2 for a two-syllable word and so on.

Compound words

Compound words are words made up of two words joined together. It can be very helpful when spelling longer words to identify the separate words within the longer word. They can be one of three types:

1 JOINED (OR SOLID) COMPOUNDS

For example: anywhere, breakdown, checkout, database, goodwill, inlet, jackpot, landmark, meantime, nowhere, ongoing, printout, redhead, schoolteacher, tablecloth, uttermost, weekend, wellbeing, yardstick

2 HYPHENATED COMPOUNDS

For example: able-bodied, back-pedal, check-in, dog-eared, empty-handed, follow-up, get-together, half-mast, in-law, jumped-up, know-how, life-size, mind-blowing, narrow-minded, one-sided, passer-by, red-hot, self-service, time-consuming, uncared-for, voice-over, well-bred, year-end

3 SEPARATE (SPACED) COMPOUNDS

For example: act up, buzz word, cash flow, drop off, evil eye, focal point, ground floor, hard shoulder, ice skate, jet engine, keep up, lay off, mass media, nod off, old maid, quarry tile, red rag, sea anchor, talk back, upper class, vegetable marrow, war cry, yellow card, zebra crossing

Some compound words can take different forms; such as:
back-up (noun); back up (verb)
working class (noun); working-class (adjective)
make-up (noun); make up (verb)
handout (noun); hand out (verb)
cut-out (noun); cut out (verb)

Words within words

Finding smaller words within longer words can be a real help with spelling. Knowing that 'friend' has 'end' in it, for example, can help you remember whether the word has 'ie' or 'ei' in the middle. Finding words within words helps to develop visual memory as well as making spelling fun!

to get her
break fast
in dig nit y
now a days
sea man ship
so me times

Sometimes stressing the word within a word that causes the most difficulty can help you remember the spelling, for example:

government
gar**den**er
envir**on**ment
or**din**ary
w**ant**ed
c**our**se
inte**rest**ing
clo**the**s
hap**pen**ed
they
y**our**
beca**use**
m**one**y
m**or**ning
every
h**ear**d
be**lie**ve
frigh**ten**ed
mo**ther**
main**ten**ance

Using dictionaries

Types of dictionaries

There is a wide range of dictionaries available today – to suit all ages and abilities and different purposes. Here are some of them:

- ❑ Acronyms and abbreviations
- ❑ Colloquialisms and slang
- ❑ Bilingual and multilingual
- ❑ Foreign language dictionaries
- ❑ Humorous dictionaries
- ❑ Encyclopaedic dictionaries
- ❑ Technical dictionaries (such as computing)
- ❑ Pronunciation dictionaries
- ❑ Thesauruses
- ❑ Picture dictionaries
- ❑ Illustrated dictionaries
- ❑ On-line dictionaries
- ❑ Idiom and phrase dictionaries
- ❑ Rhyming dictionaries
- ❑ Synonyms and antonyms
- ❑ Spelling dictionaries
- ❑ CD-Rom dictionaries
- ❑ Etymological dictionaries
- ❑ Dictionaries of proverbs
- ❑ School dictionaries
- ❑ New words dictionaries
- ❑ Crossword dictionaries
- ❑ Specialist dictionaries (such as for law and music)
- ❑ Dialect dictionaries
- ❑ Dictionaries for learners of English
- ❑ Pocket dictionaries
- ❑ Concise dictionaries
- ❑ Phonetically arranged dictionaries
- ❑ Dictionaries of grammar and English usage

It is helpful if schools can have access to an unabridged dictionary (which may contain over 450,000 entries) as a definitive reference guide. Teachers also need an abridged desk dictionary as well as multiple copies of several different types of dictionaries (for example, thesauruses and school dictionaries) that are suitable for the age level being taught.

The following dictionaries are very useful in schools:

RHYMING DICTIONARIES

Rhyming dictionaries are excellent for helping to find just the right word when writing poetry or songs. They are fun to use and encourage children to explore the sounds and forms of words. Most rhyming dictionaries have an index that refers the user to a group number in the first part of the book.

For example:

time 236

236 – ime
I'm, chyme, chime, dime, lime, climb, clime, slime, mime, rime, rhyme, crime, grime, prime, cyme, time, thyme

(Look in the index to find 'time' and then look up number 236 in the dictionary to find words that rhyme with 'time'.)

SPELLING DICTIONARIES

These dictionaries include more entries than other dictionaries of a similar size by simplifying the definitions and omitting multiple meanings and word derivations. Some spelling dictionaries do not have definitions at all and others present the word phonetically first.

The advantage of these kinds of dictionaries is that the pages are less cluttered making it easier for a less confident speller to find a word.

For example:
P   short vowel e

peck	peasant	
peg(ged)	pebble	
pelt	pedal (foot lever)	pedalling
pen(ned)	pedalled	pedestal
pence	peddle(d)	pedigree
pest	peddler	pelican
pet(ted)	peddling	penalty(ies)
		pendulum

PICTURE DICTIONARIES

Picture dictionaries are usually divided into subject sections such as food, toys, transport, flowers, dogs etc. The pictures on the page are labelled so the child can find the picture of the object they are trying to spell in order to find the word. Ideal for young children, they are also very useful for older children who may be looking for a collection of words that relate to one subject – in order to make a word search, for example.

 ball

 balloon

ILLUSTRATED DICTIONARIES

Illustrated dictionaries contain fewer words than other dictionaries of the same size and are usually set out with more spacing between the words than in a conventional dictionary. Some of the words on each page will be illustrated, making the book more appealing to younger users. The illustrations can also serve as a guide to finding the correct section of the dictionary when finding a word (as guide words at the top of the page do).

THESAURUSES

The name thesaurus comes from a Greek word meaning 'treasure' or 'treasury'. Thesauruses contain synonyms and sometimes antonyms. They are extremely useful when trying to think of an alternative word to use in our writing – to prevent the overuse of words such as 'good' and 'nice' or to find a more exciting or relevant word. They can also help us with our memory! Sometimes we can't remember a particular word but we *can* remember a word with a similar meaning. Looking up this word will often provide us with the word we were trying to remember in the first place! Thesauruses also help to expand and enrich our vocabulary by providing us with words that can express different shades of meaning.

For example: **consistent**

synonyms   1. constant, dependable, persistent, regular, steady, true to type, unchanging, undeviating; 2. accordant, agreeing, all of a piece, coherent, compatible, congruous, consonant, harmonious, logical
antonyms   1. changing, deviating, erratic, inconsistent, irregular; 2. contradictory, contrary, discordant, incompatible, incongruous, inconsistent, inharmonious

The numbers in the above example refer to different meanings of the word. When using a thesaurus you must be aware of how you want to use the word – 'harmonious', for example, could not be substituted with 'regular'.

PHONETICALLY ARRANGED DICTIONARIES

Phonetically arranged dictionaries have the words listed according to their pronunciations. They are especially useful for people with dyslexia.

Dictionary activities

1   Make a class picture dictionary that relates to the class topic. Each child could contribute a page. Older children could be asked to do quite detailed labelled diagrams/drawings.

2   Have a word hunt. Who can find the longest word in the dictionary? Who can find a word with all the vowels in it? (For example, aeronautics.) Find one one-letter word, two two-letter words, three three-letter words, four four-letter words, five five-letter words and so on.

3   Make up a quiz that relates to the class dictionaries. For example, 'What are the guide words on page 24?', 'Which word comes after fire?', 'Which word comes before pineapple?' and 'What kind of word is tooth?'

4   Have fun inventing your own words! Ask the children to look through the dictionary and join two words together to make a new word, taking into consideration the definitions! For example:
      colossalbuzz = a huge humming noise
      incognitofish = a fish in disguise
      monkeysnaffled = stolen by a monkey

5   Play charades. One child acts out a word from a selected page in the dictionary. The others look at the page and guess the word.

6   Have fun finding silly sounding words in the dictionary! For example:
      nincompoop
      fiddlesticks
      nitty-gritty
      umpteen
Create a class collection of them. Read them out loud together to cheer yourselves up!

7   Play 'Which comes first?' Write two words on the board. Ask the children to tell you which comes first in the dictionary. Check by finding the words. The first one to find the first word and read out its definition scores a point. (Insist all dictionaries remain closed until you say 'Go'!!)

Understanding an entry

When you buy or use a new dictionary it makes good sense to spend a little time reading the first few pages which explain how the dictionary is set out and what the symbols and abbreviations mean. There are often several pages of useful information at the end of dictionaries too, such as measurement conversion tables, foreign currencies, lists and abbreviations.

AN EXAMPLE OF A DICTIONARY ENTRY

this explains how to pronounce the word (usually using the IPA – International Phonetic Alphabet)

a pronunciation key is provided at the beginning of the dictionary

the number ¹ means that there is more than one entry for this word

this explains what part of speech it is – in this case, a verb

a key to abbreviations and symbols used is provided at the front of the dictionary

entry word is presented in bold to make it stand out on the page

different definitions of the word are separated by numbers

informal and slang expressions associated with the word are given together with an example demonstrating how the phrase might be used

a second entry for the word is given

some dictionaries give you the spelling of the word when endings are added

two different meanings of the same phrase are presented as 'a' and 'b'

hop¹ (hɒp) *vb.* **hopping, hopped.** **1.** to jump forwards or upwards on one foot. **2.** (of frogs, birds etc.) to move forwards in short jumps. **3.** to jump over something. **4.** *Informal.* to move quickly (in, on, out of, etc.): *hop on a bus.* **5. hop it** *Brit. slang.* to go away. ~ *n.* **6.** an instance of hopping. **7.** *Informal.* an informal dance. **8.** *Informal.* a short journey, usually in an aircraft. **9. on the hop.** *Informal.* **a.** active or busy: *he keeps me on the hop.* **b.** *Brit.* unawares or unprepared: *you've caught me on the hop.*
hop² (hɒp) *n.* a climbing plant with green conelike flowers. See also **hops.**

(from *Collins Paperback English Dictionary - Exclusive Edition*, 1994, HarperCollins Publishers)

Bigger dictionaries usually also provide the origin of the word (its root and the language from which it originated) at the end of the entry. For example, for 'hop':

Middle English *hoppen* from Old English *hoppian*; probably akin to Old English *hype*, hip. Date: before 12th century.

Finding a word

What we need to remember about the English language is that it developed from at least four other languages – Old English (Germanic), Latin, French and Greek. English words developed phonetically until the eighteenth century when an attempt was made to standardise spelling. The decision to base this on etymology rather than phonetics has presented us all with problems ever since – so we need not feel too bad about finding spelling difficult!

All entries in a dictionary are arranged in alphabetical order with each letter having its own section. Within these sections the words are also arranged alphabetically. To use a dictionary competently, then, you need to have a good knowledge of alphabetical order. For children who struggle with this, it is a good idea to make book-marks that have the 26 letters written in order.

The letter sections can be further grouped into quarters to help you decide roughly where a word will be:

> A – E = 1st quarter
> F – M = 2nd quarter
> N – S = 3rd quarter
> T – Z = 4th quarter

At the top of each page or double page there are **guide words**. The guide word on the left-hand side of the page is the first word on that page and the guide word on the right-hand side is the last word on that page. Using the guide words can help you find a word more quickly.

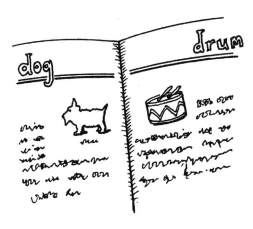

Once the correct page is found it is necessary to scan the page to find the word. Children need to be given lots of practice in scanning to prevent them from laboriously reading every word on the page.

When the word has been located, it is important to read the definition to make sure it is the word you are looking for. Some words can be spelled and pronounced the same but have different meanings (homonyms) so it is important to read the whole entry to make sure it is the word you are looking for.

Some dictionaries helpfully provide the word(s) in a sentence so that they can be seen in context.

Problems can occur when looking for a word that has a suffix added; for example, verb endings such as in the word 'omitted'. The child may not find the word because the page only lists 'omit' as an entry but the verb endings may be included in the body of the definition.

But, of course, all of this only works if you know how a word begins! Would 'ceiling' be found under 's' or 'c'?; 'chaos' sounds as if it begins with a 'k'; 'knitting' sounds as if it might begin with 'n'. Words that begin with a vowel can also cause problems if the initial sound of the word is not stressed – so if a word sounds as if it begins with a vowel and you cannot find it under one vowel, look under another. Knowing which combinations of letters can make a particular sound will help you to look up the word using various alternatives. (See below.)

consonant sound	letter(s) used
f	f (fresh); ph (physical)
g	g (goat); gh (ghost); gu (guard)
j	j (jug); g (general)
k	k (king); c (cabbage); ch (chaos)
n	n (new); kn (know); gn (gnaw); pn (pneumatic); mn (mnemonic)
r	r (run); rh (rhyme)
s	s (sun); c (ceiling); sc (scissors); ps (psychic)
sh	sh (sheen); sch (schedule); ch (chateau)
sk	sk (skill); sch (school); sc (scary)
t	t (tap); Th (Thomas) pt (pterodactyl)
w	w (wet); wh (whether)
z	z (zebra); x (xylophone) cz (czar)

Important, too, is the speed at which a word can be located. If a word cannot be found quickly the user can become easily frustrated and less likely to want to use the dictionary again.

A dictionary user, therefore, needs lots of practice in these things:

❏ locating the correct quarter of the dictionary
❏ finding the letter
❏ following the guide words
❏ finding the correct page
❏ scanning the page for the word.

Using a spellchecker

If you are using a word-processor it may come with a spell-check facility. This can be a very useful aid for spotting typing or spelling errors. Some spellcheckers automatically correct the work as you write. Some allow you to add your own words to the dictionary.

Unfortunately a spellchecker does have its limitations:

❏ It can only check those words that have been programmed into its dictionary and this number is limited.

❏ In order for the program to recognise a word, the word's spelling needs to be close to the standard. The writer will be asked to select from a list of choices for the selected word and this means they need to know how words look in order to decide which one is correct.

❏ You need to remember to make sure the spelling is the English version you require (such as UK or American). (It is interesting to note that American spelling is often closer to the original 17th century spelling in English!)

❏ It is usually unable to differentiate between words that are spelled correctly but have been used inappropriately, such as 'there' and 'their'.

You therefore need to proofread your work very carefully before accepting a final version of the writing.

Dictionary skills activities

1   Play regular quick-fire alphabetical team or group games, asking questions such as 'What letter comes before "e"?', 'What letter comes after "m"?' and 'Which letter comes first, "f" or "g"?' Score points for each correct answer.

2   Reinforce the quarter sectioning of the dictionary by playing quick games that relate to this (each child using the same dictionary). For example, 'What do the words begin with if we open the dictionary in the middle?', 'Find me a word in the first quarter.', 'What do the words start with if we open it in the last quarter?' and 'Is "territory" in the first or last quarter?'

3   Make up cards with words on them: one pack in which no two words begin with the same letter ('book', 'car', 'table'); the second pack with words that have the same initial letter but a different second letter ('mice', 'men', 'mountain'); another pack where the first and second letters are the same ('glide', 'gloom', 'glade') and so on. Challenge the children to set the words out in alphabetical order. They could time themselves to see if they can improve their times.

4   When the children are lining up, ask them to arrange themselves alphabetically according to their first or last names.

5   Play 'Guide word challenge'. Give the children two guide words, such as 'bay' and 'beam'. Ask them to think of any words that might be found on that page. How many can they think of? They could then use a dictionary to check. This game could be played in groups or teams.

6   Play 'Find the word'. Write two guide words on the board. Then write the definition of a word that is found on that page. Who can be first to find the word that belongs to that definition?

7   Challenge the children to find the differences between words of similar meaning. For example, the difference between:

   'small' and 'minuscule'
   'climate' and 'weather'
   'café' and 'restaurant'
   'pretty' and 'attractive'

Chapter 4

Spelling rules

How helpful are rules?

There can be no denying that English seems to be a very illogical language and many English words are difficult to spell but there **are** rules we can follow! In fact, most English words follow a pattern or rule, so knowing the rules can make spelling much easier.

Knowing spelling rules can help us in the following ways:

❑ Rules help us to understand the structure of our language.
❑ One rule can apply to hundreds of words.
❑ It is much easier to learn a group of words that follow the same pattern than learn how to spell each word separately.
❑ Knowing a rule can help us when we proofread our writing.

Unfortunately, there can also be problems associated with these rules:

❑ There are usually exceptions to each rule!
❑ It can be very difficult remembering the exceptions.
❑ Some rules are long and can be difficult to remember.

SOME USEFUL RULES

❑ Most people know the rule:
'i' before 'e' except after 'c'. But this is only part of the rule which may explain why it seems to have so many exceptions! The complete rule is:
'i' before 'e' except after 'c' only in words where these letters make a long 'e' sound.'

More about this rule on page 24.

❑ 'q' is always followed by 'u' and at least one vowel

❑ Every syllable has a vowel or 'y' in it.

❑ A soft 'c' or 'g' is usually followed by 'i', 'y' or 'e' (gym, city).

❑ Very few English words end in 'u' or 'i'. Words that do end in 'u' usually have a foreign origin (for example, guru – Hindi). Words that end in 'i' have a long 'e' sound (for example, 'taxi' and 'mini').

❑ Few English words end with 'j' or 'v'. ('Raj' is a Hindi word, 'guv' is an abbreviation for 'governor' and 'spiv' is a slang term.) A 'j' sound at the end of a word is represented by 'dge' or 'ge' (ledge, huge) and a 'v' sound by 've' (save, have).

❑ The 'k' sound after a short vowel is usually written as 'ck' (stack, pack), except for polysyllabic words ending in 'ic' (fantastic).

❑ When a verb and a noun sound alike, the noun usually ends in 'ice' and the verb 'ise' (practice, practise).

RULES OF COMPARISON

❑ If an adjective ends in 'y', change the 'y' into 'i' before adding 'er' or 'est' (heavy, heavier, heaviest).

❑ If an adjective ends in 'e', just add 'r' or 'st' (large, larger, largest).

❑ Some adjectives double the consonant before adding 'er' or 'est' (hot, hotter, hottest).

❑ Where the word is longer, and adding 'er' or 'est' would make it sound odd, use the words 'more' or 'most' (more careful, most recent).

Some comparatives are irregular:

bad	worse	worst
far	farther, further	farthest, furthest
good	better	best
little	lesser	least
many, much	more	most

'I' BEFORE 'E' EXCEPT AFTER 'C' BUT ONLY IN WORDS WHERE THESE LETTERS MAKE A LONG 'E' SOUND

Because this rule is so well known, it is expanded here.

When 'i' and 'e' represent a long 'e' sound:

achieve	hygiene
afield	niece
apiece	piece
belief	pier
believe	pierce
besiege	priest
bier	relief
brief	reprieve
cashier	retrieve
chief	shield
diesel	shriek
field	siege
fiend	thief
fierce	tier
frieze	wield
grief	yield
grievance	
grievous	

Exceptions: either*, caffeine, neither*, plebeian, protein, seize, seizure, sheik, Sheila.

* depending how you pronounce it

When 'i' and 'e' represent a long 'e' sound after 'c':

ceiling	deceive
conceit	perceive
conceive	receipt
deceit	receive

Exceptions: specie, species

'ei' can represent a long 'a' sound:

beige	reign
deign	rein
eight	skein
feign	veil
feint	vein
freight	weigh
inveigh	weight
neigh	
neighbour	

'ei' can represent a short 'i' sound:

foreign	sovereign
forfeit	surfeit

'ei' can represent a long 'i' sound:

eider
eiderdown
Eiger
Fahrenheit
height
sleight

'ei' can represent an 'ea(r)' sound:

weird	weir

'ei' can represent an 'ai(r)' sound:

heir	heiress
their	

'ie' can represent an 'yoo' sound:

lieu	review
view	

There are other words where 'i' and 'e' occur together and there is no long 'e' sound:

❏ When there are two separate sounds; for example, experience – ex/per/i/ence.

❏ In words when 'y' changes to 'i' in endings; for example, tiny – tiniest.

❏ In words where 'ci' makes a 'sh' sound, the 'i' comes before the 'e'; for example, ancient.

So...

if you are unsure whether it is 'ie' or 'ei', say the word and listen to the vowel sound.

If it is a long 'e', then:
it's 'ie' if there's no 'c' and
it's 'ei' if after 'c'.

If the vowel sound is a long 'a' or another sound, then it's usually 'ei'.

It is interesting to note that vowel sounds change faster than any other part of language over time (they were pronounced differently in the 1950s, for example) and that there are regional variations (for example, between northern and southern England).

Silent letters

Unfortunately, modern English contains words that have letters that are no longer pronounced (or have ceased to be pronounced as vigorously as they once were) so this can cause problems with spelling. In Old English all the letters in a word were pronounced. Some silent letters are also the result of the adoption of words from other languages.

Letters can be silent at the beginning, middle or end of words. It can be very useful when learning how to spell words with silent letters to group the words together and perhaps make up a sentence (mnemonic) to help you remember them.

(Note: there may be some debate whether the letters in the following word lists are actually silent – due to regional pronunciations, for example.)

SILENT INITIAL LETTERS

g   gnarled, gnash, gnat, gnathic, gnaw, gnome, gnomic, gnomon, gnostic (OE)

h   haute cuisine, hauteur, heir, heiress, heirloom, honest, honorarium, honorary, honour, honourable, hors d'oeuvre, hostler (F)

k   knack, knapsack, knapweed, knave, knavery, knead, knee, kneecap, kneel, knell, knelt, knew, knickerbockers, knickers, knick-knack, knife, knight, knighthood, knightly, knitting, knitwear, knives, knob, knock, knockout, knoll, knot, knot-hole, knotty, know, knowledge, known, knuckle (OE)

m   mnemonic (GK)

p   pneumatic, pneumonia, psalm, psalmist, psalmody, psalter, psaltery, psephology, pseud, pseudo-, pseudonym, psittacosis, psoriasis, psyche, psychedelic, psychiatry, psychic, psycho, psychoanalyse, psychoanalysis, psychogenic, psychological, psychology, psychopath, psychosis, psychosomatic, psychotherapy, psych-up, pterodactyl, Ptolemaic, Ptolemy, ptomaine (GK)

w   who, whodunnit, whoever, whole, wholefood, whole-hearted, wholemeal, wholesale, wholesome, wholly, whom, whomever, whooping cough, whore, whose, whosoever, wrack, wraith, wrangle, wrap, wraparound, wrapper, wrapping, wrasse, wrath, wreak, wreath, wreathe, wreck, wreckage, wrecker, wren, wrench, wrest, wrestle, wrestling, wretch, wretched, wrick, wriggle, wright, wring, wringer, wrinkle, wrist, wristwatch, writ, write, writer, writhe, writing, written, wrong, wrongdoer, wrongful, wrote, wrought, wrought iron, wrung, wry (OE)

SILENT MIDDLE LETTERS

a   extraordinary, miniature

b   bomber, bombshell, climber, debt, doubt, dumb-bell, dumbfound, dumbstruck, dumb-waiter, numbness, plumber, plumbing, plumb line, subtle, subtlety, thumbnail, thumbscrew

c   scenario, scene, scenery, scenic, scent, sceptre, sciatic, sciatica, science, scientific, scientist, scimitar, scintilla, scintillate, scissors

ch   yacht

d   budget, dredge, handkerchief, handsome, Wednesday

e   bludgeon, curmudgeon, dungeon, luncheon, omelette, pigeon, sturgeon, surgeon

g   campaign, design, diaphragm, foreign, poignant, reign, resign, sign

h   bronchitis, chronic, chronicle, exhaust, exhaustion, exhaustive, exhibit, exhibition, exhibitioner, exhibitionism, exhilarate, exhort, ghastly, ghat, ghee, gherkin, ghetto, ghillie, ghost, ghoul, ghyll, Graham, John, rhapsodize, rhapsody, rhea, rhebok, rhenium, rheostat, rhesus factor, rhetoric, rhetorical, rheum, rheumatic, rheumatism, rheumatoid, rhinestone, rhino, rhinoceros, rhizome, rhodium, rhododendron, rhombohedron, rhomboid, rhombus, rhubarb, rhyme, rhymester, rhythm, Theresa, Thomas
'wh' words such as what, when, where, why
'ch' words such as chaos, character, chemical

l   almond, calf, calfskin, calm, chalk, colonel, could, folk, folklore, folksy, half, half back, halfpenny, half-tone, halfway, halfwit, Lincoln, palm, palmistry, palmy, psalm, psalmist, psalmody, salmon, should, talk, would, yolk

p   corps, cupboard, raspberry, receipt

s   aisle, island, islander, isle, islet

t   accepts, acts, batch, blotch, botch, castle, catch, chestnut, christen, Christmas, clutch, crotch, crutch, ditch, ducts, fasten, hatch, hitch, hustle, hutch, kitchen, latch, lifts, listen, match, mortgage, mustn't, notch, often, patch, pitch, rustle, scratch, soften, switch, thatch, thistle, whistle, witch

th   asthma, isthmus

u biscuit, buoy, buoyant, guarantee, guarantor, guaranty, guard, guardhouse, guardian, guardsman, Guernsey, guerrilla, guess, guesswork, guest, guest-house, guidance, guide, guidebook, guideline, guild, guilder, guildhall, guile, guillemot, guillotine, guilt, guiltless, guilty, guinea, guinea pig, guipure, guise, guitar

w answer, answerable, playwright, sword, swordfish, swordplay, swordsman, sword-stick, two, wheelwright

SILENT FINAL LETTERS

b aplomb, bomb, climb, comb, crumb, dumb, limb, numb, plumb, thumb, tomb (OE)

n autumn, column, condemn, damn, hymn, solemn (OE)

s Arkansas, bourgeois, debris, Illinois (US/F)

t ballet, buffet, chalet, crochet, debut, depot, gourmet, valet (F)

SILENT OR MAGIC 'E'

The rule for silent 'e' words is:

When a word ends in silent 'e' the earlier vowel says its name instead of its sound.

Unfortunately, this rule doesn't apply to short vowel words such as 'give', 'gone' and 'have'. So it is important to be aware of this and to learn about the two categories of silent 'e' words:

❑ those that have a long vowel in the middle (that says its name), such as:
atone, bite, cute, date, excite, fine, gave, hate, joke, kite, lope, mine, nave, pane, quake, ride, sire, time, unable, vine, wane, yoke, zone

❑ those that have a short vowel in the middle (that says its short sound), such as:
done, force, give, have, one, some, there, where

What happens to the silent 'e' when suffixes are added is dealt with in Chapter 7.

Silent letter activities

1 Make up some cards with words on them that have silent letters in them. Ask the children to group them into sets with the same silent letter. They could also play snap where they match words that have the same silent letter.

2 Help the children to develop visual memory skills by carrying out activities where they have to recognise the incorrect spelling amongst correct ones; for example:

knitting	kitchen
knew	cuboard
head	gnaw
knack	wreck

3 Ask the children to use dictionaries to find words with a particular silent letter. Who can find the most words? Put the words on display as a word chart or part of a silent letter word wall that can be added to over several weeks.

4 Have fun trying to remember words with silent letters by asking the children to make up sentences or alliterations; for example:

With much aplomb the dumb climber dropped his comb which fell like a bomb onto his limb which broke his thumb into little crumbs that fell onto the tomb below.

Knobbly knights knitted knockout knotty knitwear knickers knowledgably.

HARD AND SOFT 'C' AND 'G'

'c' and 'g' usually make a soft sound when followed by 'e', 'i' or 'y'.

A soft 'c' (sounding like an 's') is more usual in the middle and end of a word than at the beginning; for example:

absence, ace, acid, advance, announce, balance, bodice, bounce, brace, confidence, conspiracy, convince, currency, dance, December, defence, dice, entrance, exceed, excel, excellent, except, excess, fancy, fence, ferocity, finance, frequency, glance, grace, grocer, hacienda, homicide, hospice, ice, icing, icy, ignorance, imbecile, innocent, insurance, juice, juicy, justice, lace, lacerate, lacing, lance, lancet, lattice, lucerne, lyceum, mace, magnificent, malice, medicine, mice, mince, necessary, nice, once, ordinance, ordnance, pace, parcel, peace, penance, pence, penicillin, perceive, percentage, perceptive, place, Pleiocene, practice, price, prince, principle, proceed, province, puce, quince, race, receive, recess, recipe, recipient, recital, recite, reliance, reminiscence, renounce, replace, resource, rhinoceros, rice, romance, sentence, sequence, service, since, slice, sluice, society, solace, space, specific, specimen, spice, spicy, supercilious, tercel, terrace, thrice, trace, trice, turbulence, twice, ulcer, uncertain, vacillate, valance, vice, vicious, wince, winceyette, Worcester

This rule helps us to understand that both 'c' and 's' can make an 's' sound so this gives us another option when trying to spell a word. It also helps to pronounce unfamiliar words.

Examples of soft 'c' at the beginning of a word:

Caesar, Caesarean, caesium, cease, cedar, ceiling, celebrate, celery, cell, cellar, cellular, Celsius, cement, cemetery, cenotaph, census, cent, centenary, centimetre, centipede, central, centre, century, ceramic, cereal, ceremony, certain, certificate, certify, cider, cigar, cilium, cinder, cinema, cinnamon, cipher, circle, circuit, circulate, circumference, circumstance, circus, cistern, cite, citizen, citric, citrus, city, civic, civil, cycle, cyclone, Cyclops, cygnet, cylinder, cymbal, cyst

In words with two 'c's together, the first 'c' makes a hard sound and the second is soft; for example:

accident, eccentric, vaccination

The soft 'g' rule at the beginning of words is not as reliable the as soft 'c' rule because there are quite a few words that have 'g' followed by 'e', 'i' or 'y' that have a hard sound; for example:

gear, geese, get, giddy, girl, give

Examples of soft 'g' in the middle of words:

advantageous, agent, agile, agitate, angel, angina, biogenesis, biology, budgerigar, budget, budgie, codger, contagious, contingency, contingent, courageous, degenerate, dungeon, Egyptian, engagement, evangelical, flagellum, fledgling, Georgian, hedgehog, hodgepodge, homogenise, homogenous, hydrogen, hydrogenate, hygiene, ideology, imagery, imagination, imagine, indulgence, judgement, kedgeree, knowledgeable, largess, legend, legible, legion, legionnaire, legislate, legitimate, magenta, magic, magician, magistrate, manger, mangetout, margarine, margin, menagerie, meningitis, messenger, microbiology, microsurgery, midget, octogenarian, oestrogen, orangeade, orangery, origin, original, outrageous, pageant, page-boy, passageway, phonology, refrigerator, refugee, regency, regenerate, regent, regime, regiment, region, register, sergeant, staging, stranger, tangible, terminology, tragedy, tragic, trilogy, turgid, urgent, vegetable, vengeance, vigil, vigilant, wager, zoology

Examples of soft 'g' at the end of words:

age, badge, barge, barrage, beige, besiege, beverage, bodge, bondage, bulge, cabbage, cadge, camouflage, carnage, carriage, cartilage, change, college, corsage, courage, cribbage, damage, disadvantage, discharge, discourage, disengage, disparage, dodge, drainage, edge, engage, enlarge, espionage, estrange, exchange, flange, fledge, foliage, footage, forage, fringe, frontage, gage, garage, garbage, greengage, hedge, herbage, homage, image, indulge, kedge, knowledge, large, ledge, lodge, luggage, manage, manège, mange, massage, merge, message, midge, montage, nudge, oblige, orange, outrage, page, parsonage, passage, peerage, pilgrimage, pledge, plunge, porridge, privilege, rage, rampage, refuge, ribcage, sage, salvage, savage, sedge, shortage, siege, silage, stage, storage, strange, syringe, urge, usage, verge, wage, wedge, whinge

Examples of soft 'g' at the beginning of words:

> gem, general, generous, genie, genuine, geography, geometry, Georgian, germ, gesture, giant, gibber, gibberish, gibbet, gibe, giblets, gigantic, gin, ginger, ginormous, ginseng, gip, gipsy, giraffe, giro, gist

The apostrophe

The main uses of the apostrophe are:

- ❏ To show that letters are missing (contractions); for example, he'll = he will.
- ❏ To indicate the owner (possession); for example, 'the boy's book'. This does not apply to pronouns such as 'his', 'its', 'yours' and 'hers'.

It is very important to remember that apostrophes are **not** used to make words plural.

CONTRACTIONS

Contractions are the easiest form of the apostrophe to use, although sometimes children put the apostrophe in the wrong place; for example 'had'nt' (hadn't) instead of where the letter has been omitted. And one of the most common mistakes in spelling is to use 'it's' (it is) to mean the possessive 'its'.

Some forms of contractions are more unusual:

> shan't = shall not
> won't = will not

The shortened forms of words are best used for conversations and informal writing. The longer forms should be used for all other writing.

POSSESSION

❏ Singular
To form the possessive of a singular noun, add apostrophe 's'. For example, 'The girl's bike'. For some singular nouns, especially names, it is correct to add either an apostrophe or apostrophe 's', depending on the length of the word. Usually you add apostrophe 's' for a single syllable name – 'Charles's bike', and either form for a longer word – 'Hastings' beach, 'Dumas's book'.

❏ Plural
To form the possessive of a plural noun, add the apostrophe after the 's'. For example, 'The girls' bikes'. If the word does not end in an 's', then add apostrophe 's'. For example, 'The men's bikes.'

❏ Group
If there are joint possessors of a single object or thing, the apostrophe 's' is added to the last of them. For example, 'William and Mary's bike'.

But if William and Mary have separate bikes, instead of a shared one, it will become 'William's and Mary's bikes'.

❏ Compound or hyphenated words
In compound or hyphenated words, the apostrophe 's' is added to the last part of it. For example, 'The mother-in-law's bike'.

Capital letters

There are specific rules about when to use capital, or upper case, letters. These are:

1 AT THE BEGINNING OF SENTENCES

A capital letter is always used at the beginning of a sentence, so a full stop is usually followed by a capital letter. An exclamation mark and a question mark are also followed by a capital except in direct speech (see below).

2 IN DIRECT SPEECH

A capital is used for the first word in direct speech; for example:

> Sally said 'Please sit down.'

A capital is not used after an exclamation mark or question mark in direct speech; for example:

> 'Why did you go there?' asked Mike.

3 IN POETRY

The first word of each line of verse usually starts with a capital letter: for example:

> Five old fishermen
> Sitting on a bridge,
> One caught a tiddler,
> One caught a fridge.

4 FOR PROPER NOUNS OR ADJECTIVES

Capitals are used for proper names and adjectives of people, places, brands, religions, days, months, compass points, companies and organisations, titles of people, books and films and so on. For example:

Scotland, Queen Victoria, Bath (nouns)
Scottish, Victorian, Bathonian (adjectives)
Ford, Jaguar, Coca-Cola
Judaism, Protestant, Buddhist
General Motors Company
High Street, London Road

Exceptions – lower case is used for 'roman' typefaces and 'arabic' numerals.

All words in a title except the subsidiary words, hence:

the House of Lords
Archbishop of Canterbury
Vale of Evesham
Gone with the Wind

Verbs of national and regional affiliations also normally use capitals; for example, 'Anglicise'.

Capitals are not used for compass directions, such as north-east, but are used when describing a geographical location; for example, 'in the North-East'.

5 FOR THE PRONOUN 'I'

The pronoun 'I' always has a capital letter.

Short and long vowels

Understanding the vowels

Vowel sounds in words are represented by the letters a, e, i, o, u and sometimes y. These letters can make different sounds in words (for example, the 'a' in man, baby and was) and the pronunciation can also vary according to geographical regions.

Two or more vowels can also be combined to produce different vowel sounds; for example, the 'ee' in 'meet' and the 'ea' in 'meat' both make the same sound and yet the 'ea' in 'head' makes another different sound!

Clusters of vowels and consonants in larger spelling patterns can also represent vowel sounds (for example, 'igh' in 'might') and these clusters can also make different sounds in words; for example, the 'ough' in 'cough', 'though', 'plough' and 'rough'.

And this is why the spelling of English words can be so tricky! And why it is so important to learn about the various combinations that can make the different sounds.

Short vowel sounds

The short vowel sound is what the letter 'says'. For example:

> 'a' as in apple
> 'e' as in egg
> 'i' as in igloo
> 'o' as in orange
> 'u' as in umbrella
>
> 'y' as in gym

A vowel is short if the syllable ends in one or more consonants (a closed syllable). For example:

pencil	pen/cil
buttress	but/tress
kitten	kit/ten
fledgling	fledg/ling

RULES FOR CLOSED SYLLABLES

❏ The consonants 'f', 'l', 's' and 'z' are usually doubled at the end of short vowel one-syllable words. For example:
> bluff
> fell
> moss
> buzz

But there are a few exceptions, such as 'if', 'of', 'is', 'this', 'thus', 'his', 'bus', 'us' and 'has'.

❏ Rules for using 'ck' or 'k' at the end of words of one syllable. Use:

a) 'ck' at the end if it is a short vowel sound with no other consonant sound before the final 'k' sound. For example:

> brick
> sick
> snack

Exception: trek

b) 'k' at the end of a word if there is another consonant sound before the final 'k' sound (or if there is a long vowel sound). For example:

> tank
> link
> silk

❏ Rules for using 'dge' or 'ge' at the end of words of one syllable. Use:

a) 'dge' at the end if it is a short vowel sound with no other consonant sound before the final 'j' sound. For example:

> badge
> lodge
> nudge

b) 'ge' at the end of a word if there is another consonant sound before the final 'j' sound. For example:

> bulge
> cringe
> merge

❏ Rules for using 'tch' or 'ch' at the end of words of one syllable. Use:

a) 'tch' at the end if it is a short vowel sound with no other consonant sound before the final 'ch' sound. For example:

> fetch
> hitch
> clutch

b) 'ch' at the end of a word if there is another consonant sound before the final 'ch' sound (or a long vowel sound). For example:

> drench
> pinch
> winch

TWO VOWELS COMBINING TO MAKE A SHORT VOWEL SOUND (DIPHTHONG)

Normally, it is only one vowel that makes a short vowel sound but there are some occasions when two vowels combine to make a single short vowel sound:

❑ 'ie' and 'ei' making a short 'e' sound
   For example: friend, leisure

❑ 'ie' making a short 'i' sound
   For example: mischief, sieve

❑ 'ea' making a short 'e' sound
   For example: bread, death, peasant, tread

❑ 'ui' making a short 'i' sound
   For example: build, guilt, guinea

❑ 'au' making a short 'o' sound
   For example: Australia, laurel, sausage

❑ 'ou' making a short 'u' sound
   For example: courage, double, young

Useful family word groups

SHORT 'A' WORDS

b**ad**, dad, fad, had, lad, mad, pad, sad

b**ag**, lag, nag, rag, tag, wag

am, bam, dam, ham, jam, ram

an, ban, can, fan, man, nan, pan, ran, tan, van

b**ap**, cap, gap, lap, map, nap, rap, sap, tap, yap

at, bat, cat, fat, hat, mat, pat, rat, sat, tat, vat

b**ack**, hack, jack, lack, nack, pack, rack, sack, tack, attack, black, crack, jacket, packet, quack, snack, stack, track

act, fact, pact, tact, action, active, actor, actress, actual, attract, tractor, practice, practise

l**amb**, amble, amber, ambition, ambulance, ambush, bramble, gamble, ramble, shambles, scramble

c**amp**, damp, lamp, ramp, vamp, ample, champion, clamp, cramp, example, sample, stamp

and, band, hand, land, sand, abandon, handsome, island, sandals

b**ang**, fang, gang, hang, pang, rang, sang, tang, angle, angry, sprang, triangle

b**ank**, dank, lank, rank, sank, tank, yank, ankle, blank, blanket, drank, plank, thank

ash, bash, cash, dash, lash, mash, rash, sash, ashamed, ashore, crash, smash, splash, thrash, trash

b**atch**, catch, hatch, latch, match, patch, scratch, snatch, thatch

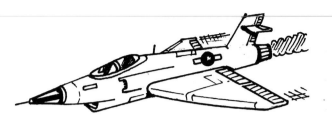

SHORT 'E' WORDS

b**ed**, fed, led, red, wed, zed

b**eg**, keg, leg, peg

d**en**, fen, hen, men, pen, ten, when

b**et**, get, jet, let, met, net, pet, set, vet, wet

b**eck**, deck, heck, neck, peck, speck, wreck

s**ect**, correct, elect, electric, expect, inspect, object, perfect, protect, respect, select, subject

b**ell**, cell, dell, fell, hell, sell, tell, well, dwell, shell, smell, spell, swell

b**elt**, celt, felt, melt, pelt, welt, smelt, spelt, shelter, swelter

b**end**, fend, lend, mend, send, tend, blend, friend, pretend, tender

b**ent**, cent, dent, gent, lent, pent, rent, sent, tent, vent, went, comment, event, plenty, present, spent, twenty

k**ept**, wept, crept, slept, swept

b**est**, nest, pest, rest, test, vest, west, zest, arrest, contest, inquest, invest, orchestra, protest, question, request

SHORT 'I' WORDS

b**id**, did, hid, kid, lid, rid

b**ig**, dig, fig, pig, rig, wig

in, bin, din, fin, gin, kin, pin, sin, tin, win

d**ip**, hip, kip, lip, nip, pip, rip, sip, tip

it, bit, fit, hit, kit, lit, mitt, nit, pit, sit, wit

h**ick**, kick, lick, nick, pick, rick, sick, tick, wick, brick, quick, stick, thick, trick

m**iff**, riff, tiff, cliff, difficult, sniff, sniffle, stiff, whiff

g**ift**, lift, rift, sift, adrift, drift, fifty, shift, swift

ill, bill, dill, fill, gill, hill, kill, mill, pill, rill, sill, till, will

ink, dink, fink, link, mink, pink, rink, sink, wink, drink, shrink, think

d**itch**, hitch, pitch, titch, witch, kitchen, stitch, switch

SHORT 'O' WORDS

c**od**, god, nod, pod, rod

b**og**, dog, fog, hog, jog, log

b**op**, cop, hop, lop, mop, pop, sop, top

c**ot**, dot, got, hot, jot, lot, not, pot, rot, tot

d**ock**, hock, jock, lock, mock, rock, sock, tock, block, clock, stock

b**oss**, doss, loss, moss, toss, across, cross, floss, gloss

SHORT 'U' WORDS

c**ub**, dub, hub, nub, pub, rub, sub, tub

b**ud**, cud, dud, mud, stud

b**ug**, dug, hug, jug, lug, mug, pug, rug, tug

b**un**, fun, gun, nun, pun, run, sun, Sunday

b**ut**, cut, gut, hut, jut, nut, rut, tut, butter, shutter

b**uck**, duck, luck, muck, puck, ruck, suck, tuck, bucket, struck, stuck, truck

d**umb**, numb, crumb, grumble, jumble, mumble, number, plumber, rumble, slumber, stumble, thumb

b**ump**, dump, hump, jump, lump, pump, rump, sump, mumps, stump

b**ust**, dust, gust, just, must, rust, cluster, crust, industry, rustle, thrust, trust

Long vowel sounds

The long vowel sound is the letter's name.
For example:

'a' as in ace
'e' as in me
'i' as in find
'o' as in go
'u' as in music

'y' as in by

A vowel is long if the syllable ends in a single vowel (open syllable). For example:

cable   ca/ble
motor   mo/tor
photo   pho/to
ideal   i/deal

MAGIC 'E' WORDS

When a word such as 'can', 'pin', 'not' or 'cub' has an 'e' added to the end, it now has two vowels and 'magically' the first vowel changes from short to long – 'cane', 'pine', 'note' and 'cube'. This silent 'e' pattern occurs most often in words of more than one syllable and in different positions in words but it is more likely to be found at the end of words. For example:

space/craft
sur/vive
in/ter/face

TWO VOWELS COMBINING TO MAKE A LONG VOWEL SOUND

❏ 'ai' making a long 'a' sound
For example: 'aim', 'straight', 'train'

❏ 'ee' making a long 'e' sound
For example: 'bee', 'keep', 'committee'

❏ 'ea' making a long 'e' sound
For example: 'eat', 'meal', 'weave'

❏ 'oa' making a long 'o' sound
For example: 'oak', 'coat', 'poach'

❏ 'oe' making a long 'o' sound
For example: 'doe', 'foe', 'toe'

❏ 'ow' making a long 'o' sound
For example: 'bow', 'owe', 'throw'

❏ 'ue' making a long 'u' sound
For example: 'blue', 'cue', 'true'

❏ 'oo' making a long 'u' sound
For example: 'boo', 'balloon', 'school'

❏ 'ew' making a long 'u' sound
For example: 'dew', 'flew', 'shrew'

❏ 'ou' making a long 'u' sound
For example: 'soup', 'route', 'youth'

❏ 'ui' making a long 'u' sound
For example: 'fruit', 'juice', 'suitable'

❏ 'eu' making a long 'u' sound
For example: 'feud', 'sleuth'

OTHER LONG VOWEL SOUNDS

❏ 'ay' makes a long 'a' sound at the end of words.
For example: 'bay', 'clay', 'today'

❏ 'ey' or 'y' makes a long 'e' sound at the end of words.
For example: 'happy', 'donkey', 'stony'

❏ 'igh' makes a long 'i' sound.
For example: 'sigh', 'might', 'flight'

Useful family word groups

LONG 'A' WORDS – A-E

ace, dace, face, lace, mace, pace, race, grace, place, replace, space, trace

fade, jade, made, wade, blade, glade, grade, parade, shade, spade, trade

age, cage, page, rage, sage, wage, stage

bake, cake, fake, hake, lake, make, rake, sake, take, wake, awake, baker, brake, flake, mistake, shake, snake, stake

ale, bale, dale, gale, hale, kale, male, pale, sale, tale, vale, stale, Wales, whale

came, dame, fame, game, lame, name, same, tame, became, blame, flame, frame, shame

bane, cane, Dane, Jane, lane, mane, pane, sane, vane, wane, crane, insane, plane

ape, cape, gape, jape, nape, tape, shape

base, case, basement, chase, phrase

ate, date, fate, gate, hate, late, mate, rate, sate, decorate, later, separate

cave, Dave, gave, nave, pave, rave, save, wave, behave, brave, pavement, slave

daze, gaze, haze, laze, maze, blaze, craze, graze

LONG 'A' WORDS – AY

bay, day, gay, hay, jay, lay, may, nay, pay, ray, say, way, betray, bray, clay, dismay, display, pray, spray, stray, sway, tray

able, cable, fable, gable, sable, table

nation, examination, information, invitation, plantation, population, separation, station, vacation

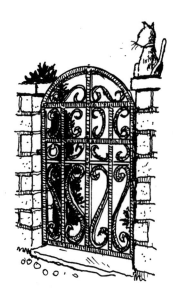

LONG 'A' WORDS – AI

aid, laid, maid, paid, raid, afraid

ail, bail, fail, hail, jail, mail, nail, pail, rail, sail, tail, wail, daily, frail, snail, trail

aim, maim, claim, exclaim, proclaim

gain, lain, main, pain, rain, vain, brain, chain, drain, explain, grain, remain, sprain, stain, train

LONG 'E' WORDS – EE

bee, fee, gee, lee, pee, see, tee, wee, zee, free, tree

deed, feed, heed, need, reed, seed, weed, bleed, breed, greed, needle, speed, tweed, weedy

leek, meek, peek, reek, seek, week, creek

eel, feel, heel, peel, reel, steel, wheel

been, keen, seen, between, green, preen, queen, screen

beep, deep, jeep, peep, seep, weep, asleep, cheep, creep, sheep, sleep, steep, sweep

feet, meet, fleet, sheet, sleet, street, sweet, tweet

breeze, freeze, squeeze, sneeze, tweezers, wheeze

LONG 'E' WORDS – EA

l**ea**, pea, sea, tea, flea

b**ead**, lead, read, leader, plead

b**eak**, leak, teak, weak, creak, freak, sneak, speak, streak

d**eal**, heal, meal, peal, real, seal, teal, veal, weal, zeal, steal

b**eam**, ream, seam, team, cream, dream, gleam, ice-cream, scream, steam, stream

b**ean**, lean, mean, wean, clean, cleaner

h**eap**, leap, reap, cheap

b**eat**, feat, heat, meat, neat, peat, seat, teat, wheat

LONG 'E' WORDS – Y

an**y**, bury, cherry, dolly, every, ferry, golly, happy, icy, jelly, kitty, lorry, merry, nippy, only, poppy, quarry, ready, sleepy, teddy, unsteady, very, wispy, yappy, zany

LONG 'E' WORDS – ETE

athl**ete**, Crete, complete, compete, concrete, delete, obsolete

LONG 'E' WORDS – EACH

b**each**, peach, reach, teach, breach, bleach, teacher

LONG 'E' WORDS – EASE

easel, tease, disease, please, weasel

LONG 'E' WORDS – EAST

b**east**, feast, least, yeast, eastern

LONG 'I' WORDS – I–E

ice, dice, lice, mice, nice, rice, vice, advice, price, slice, spice, slice, twice

b**ide**, hide, ride, side, tide, wide, aside, beside, bride, glide, pride, provide

l**ife**, rife, wife, knife, strife

b**ike**, dike, hike, like, mike, pike, spike, strike, trike

b**ile**, file, mile, Nile, pile, rile, tile, vile, wile, awhile, smile, stile, while

d**ime**, lime, mime, rime, time, chime, crime, grime, prime, slime

f**ine**, line, mine, nine, pine, sine, vine, wine, shine, shrine, spine, swine, twine

p**ipe**, ripe, wipe, stripe, swipe, tripe

b**ite**, kite, mite, rite, site, white, contrite, despite, invite, respite

d**ive**, five, hive, live, alive, arrive, drive, knives

LONG 'I' WORDS – Y

b**y**, my, cry, dry, fly, fry, try, shy, sky, spy, sty, style, type

LONG 'I' WORDS – IGH

h**igh**, nigh, sigh, blight, bright, delight, fight, flight, knight, light, might, right, sight, slight, tight

LONG 'I' WORDS – IGN

s**ign**, align, design, resign

LONG 'O' WORDS – O-E

lobe, robe, strobe

bode, code, lode, mode, node, rode, strode

coke, joke, poke, woke, awoke, bloke, broke, choke, evoke, smoke, spoke, stroke

bole, cole, dole, hole, mole, pole, role, sole, vole, stole, whole

dome, home, Rome, aerodrome, gnome

bone, cone, hone, lone, tone, zone, alone, lonely, phone, stone, telephone

cope, dope, hope, lope, mope, pope, rope, grope, slope

hose, nose, pose, rose, chose, close, prose, those

dote, note, rote, tote, vote, wrote

cove, hove, clover, Dover, drove, overalls

LONG 'U' WORDS – U-E

cube, tube

dude, nude, rude, attitude, crude, denude, exclude, interlude, latitude, seclude, solitude

duke, Luke, puke, fluke, jukebox

mule, rule, yule, capsule, ruler, yuletide

fume, flume, consume, costume, exhume, perfume, plume, presume, resume, volume

dune, June, rune, tune, prune

use, fuse, muse, ruse, accuse, amuse, confuse, defuse, refuse

cute, jute, lute, mute, absolute, astute, brute, commute, compute, destitute, dispute, flute, resolute, salute

LONG 'U' WORDS – OO

boo, coo, goo, moo, poo, roo, too, woo, zoo

food, mood, brood

cool, fool, pool, tool, school, spool, stool

boon, goon, moon, noon, soon, baboon, balloon, cocoon, harpoon, spoon, swoon

coop, hoop, loop, poop, droop, nincompoop, scoop, sloop, snoop, stoop, swoop

boot, coot, hoot, loot, root, toot, scoot

goose, loose, moose, noose, choose

booth, tooth, smooth

LONG 'O' WORDS – OE

doe, foe, hoe, roe, toe, woe

LONG 'O' WORDS – OA

oak, oat, boat, coal, coat, coax, foal, foam, goal, goat, load, loan, moan, road, roam, soak, soap, cloak, coach, croak, float, groan, poach, roast, shoal, stoat, throat, toast

LONG 'U' WORDS – UE

cue, due, rue, sue, blue, clue, cruel, duel, glue, rescue, statue, true, Tuesday

LONG 'O' WORDS – OW

bow, low, mow, row, sow, tow, blow, flow, grow, glow, show, slow, snow, throw, bungalow, sparrow, swallow, tomorrow, yellow

LONG 'U' WORDS – EW

dew, few, hew, mew, new, pew, yew, blew, brew, chew, crew, drew, grew, screw, shrew, stew, threw

Spelling activities – long and short vowel sounds

1 Make up some 'Ladder' games. Make some card ladders with separate strips of card with words on them that can form the 'rungs'. The words for one game could be either long or short 'a' sounds; another can be long and short 'e' words and so on. The children can play the game in pairs. They set the ladders out and put the word rungs in a pile face down. They take it in turns to pick up a rung, say the word and decide whether it has a long or a short vowel sound. If their partner agrees with their answer, they put the rung on the correct ladder. If not, the rung goes on the bottom of the pile.

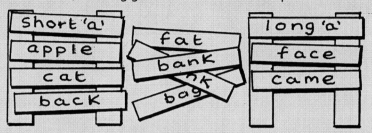

2 Make up two class word walls where the children collect words with short and long vowels in them and write the words on the appropriate wall. This activity can be extended to collecting words with a particular letter pattern, for example 'and' words.

3 Make up nonsense rhymes and jingles where the children have fun with the sounds of words.
For example:

> bat, cat … rat, mat, sat
> I saw a rat sitting on a cat
>
> lap, map … nap, rap, gap
> I saw a cap sitting on a tap

4 Play 'Word sorts'. Give the children words on cards or a list of words. Ask them to find the words with the chosen long or short vowel sound. You could also give the words to them and challenge them to work out how they could sort them – can they recognise that most of the words have a the same sound in them?

5 Make up word searches or crossword puzzles where all the words have the same long or short vowel sound.

6 Make some word trees for the children to complete, where each 'leaf' contains a word with a particular vowel sound.

Prefixes

What are prefixes?

A prefix is a letter or group of letters added to the beginning of a base word or root. A prefix changes the meaning of a word. Prefixes are usually used to indicate the opposite meaning of a word. For example, safe – **un**safe.

Many prefixes have Greek, Latin or Old English origins. Knowing about prefixes can help us with spelling because it makes it easier to build up and spell longer words. Knowing the meaning of a prefix can also help us work out the meaning of an unfamiliar word.

PREFIX RULES

1 The spelling of a base word does not change if a prefix is added. For example, mis + spell = misspell.

2 When 'all' is added to a word, one 'l' is always dropped. For example, all + ways = always. But note that 'all right' is two words (although 'alright' is used it is considered less acceptable).

3 When 'well' is added to a word, one 'l' is dropped, except in hyphenated words. For example, welcome and well-off.

4 The prefix 'in' is never used before the letters 'b', 'm' or 'p' ('im' is used instead). Before 'l', 'in' becomes 'il' and before 'r', 'in' becomes 'ir'. Hence: impossible, illegal, irregular.

5 The root 'ceed' or 'cede' (to go) can combine with a large number of prefixes. A rhyme can help to remember which to use:
    With 'suc', 'ex' and 'pro'
    Double 'e' must go
For example: succeed, exceed and proceed.

Knowing the meaning of the prefix also helps; for example, **anti** or **ante**. These sound the same but they have different meanings. 'Anti' is from the Greek for 'opposed' or 'opposite'. 'Ante' is from the Latin meaning 'before'. Hence 'antidote' and 'antenatal'.

*Note: words in italics are of Greek origin. Others are Latin or as marked (OE – Old English; F – French).

Number prefixes

Prefix	Meaning	Examples
hemi semi	half	hemisphere semicircle
mono uni	one	unicycle, unity monologue, monorail
di, dis bi, bis, duo	two	bivalve, duologue dialogue
tri, tri	three	tricycle, triangle
tetra quad, quadri	four	quadrangle, quadrille tetrahedron
penta quint(us)	five	quintet, pentagon
hex[1] ses, sex[1]	six	sestet, sextuplets hexagon
hepta sept(em)	seven	septet, heptagon
octo, oct	eight	octagon, octopus
nonus	nine	nonagon, nonagenarian
deca, decem	ten	decade, decalogue
dodeca	twelve	dodecagon dodecahedron
cent(um), centi	hundred	century, centipede
mille (F), *kilo*	thousand	millennium, kilobyte
milli	thousandth	milligram

[1] Note: the Greek guttural 'h' as in 'hex' was modified by Latin to the 's' sound; hence 'hex' became 'sex' in Latin (also hepta, septem).

Common prefixes

Prefix	Meaning	Examples	Prefix	Meaning	Examples
a, an (OE)	a negative, not, / on, in	amoral, atheist / afloat, asleep	*dys*	hard, bad, difficult	dysfunction, dyslexia
ab	away from	absent, abnormal	*ec, ex* / e, ex	out of, from, away	emit, exclude, exhale, exceed
ad	to, towards	addition	*ecto*	outside	ectoplasm
aero	air	aeroplane, aerosol	equi (aequus)	equal	equidistant, equinox
after (OE)	later, behind	afternoon, afterwards	*en, em* / em, en	in, into, cover	embed, embody, encase, enfold
al (OE)	all	always, altogether	*endo*	within	endoscope
ambi	both	ambidextrous	*epi*	on, upon	epicentre, epidural
ante	before, in front of	antenatal, anteroom	extra	outside, in addition to	extraordinary, extracurricular
anti	against	antibody, antisocial	flex(us)	bent	flexible
aqua	water	aquatic, aqualung	*geo*	earth	geography. geology
audi(o)	to hear	auditory, audible	*hetero*	other	heterosexual
auto	self	autobiography, automatic	*homo*	same	homophone
be (OE)	make, thoroughly	bedecked, belittle	*hydro*	water	hydroelectric
bene	good, well	benefit, benevolent	*hyper*	over, above	hyperactive, hypersensitive
bi, bis	twice, two	bicycle, biennial	*hypo*	below, under	hypoallergenic, hypocaust
cata	down, under	catacomb	il	not	illegal, illegible
chron(o)	time	chronicle, chronology	im, in (OE)	into, not	impolite, incurable
circum	around	circumference	infra	below	infrastructure
co	joint	co-star, cooperate	inter	between, among	interact, international
com, con	with, together	combine, conjoin	ir	not	irregular, irrational
contra	against	contradict, contrary	*macro*	large	macrobiotics
counter	against, opposite	counteract, counterproductive	magnus	great	magnify, magnificent
cred(ulus)	to believe	credible, credit	*mega*	huge	megabucks, megaton
cyclos	circle, wheel	cycle, cyclical	*meso*	middle	Mesolithic, mesosphere
de	downward, undo, away	deflate, deploy, detach	*meta*	beyond, change	metamorphosis, metaphysics
deus, div(inus)	god	deity, divine	*micro*	small	microbe, microscope
dis	apart, not	dislike, disconnect	mis (OE)	wrongly	mistake, mistreat
			miss (mittere)	to send	missile, missive

Common prefixes (cont)

Prefix	Meaning	Examples
mono	alone	monocle, monorail
morph(e)	shape	morphology
multi	many	multiply, multitude
non	not	non abrasive
omni	all	omniscient, omnivore
over (OE)	above, beyond	overflow, overhead
para	alongside	paramilitary, paramedic
per	through, thorough	perforate, persistent
peri	around, near	peripheral, periscope
phon(e)	sound	phonics, phonograph
photo	light	photograph, photon
poly	many	polygon, polygamy
port(abilis)	to carry	portable, porter
post	after	post-operative, postscript
pre	before, prior to	pre-empt, preheat, prehistoric
prim(us)	first	primal, primary
pro, *pro*	before, in favour of	proactive, propose
radio (radius)	ray, beam	radiology, radio
re	again	redo, repeat, revise
retro	backwards	retroactive, retrograde
sanctus	holy	sanctify, sanctuary
sectum	cut	section, sector
semi	half	semicircle, semitone
spectare	to look	spectacles, spectator
sub	under, below	subaltern, submarine
super, supra	above, beyond	supersede, suprarenal
sus	under	sustain, susceptible

Prefix	Meaning	Examples
syn	with, together	syndicate, synthesis
tele	distance, from afar	telecommunications, telescope, telecast
theos	god	theist, theology
tract(us)	to drag, draw	tractor, traction
trans	across	transcontinental, transfer
tri, *tri*	three	triangle, tricycle
ultra	beyond	ultramodern
un (OE)	not	unclean, untidy
under (OE)	below	underlay, underneath
uni	one	unicorn, unicycle
veho, vectum	to carry	vehicle, vector
video	see	video, videotext
vita	life	vital, vitality

tripod

triceps

triangles

triathlon

tri

tricycle

trivet

trilogy

trident

Useful words lists

Negative prefixes

'Un' is the most common prefix used to indicate a negative. It can occur with verbs (undo), adjectives (unhelpful) and adverbs (unselfishly). 'Un' derives from Old English and its Latin equivalents include 'en' and 'in'.

UN

unabashed, unable, unaccompanied, unaccountable, unaccustomed, unaffected, unannounced, unanswerable, unapproachable, unarmed, unassuming, unattached, unattended, unavoidable, unaware, unbalanced, unbearable, unbecoming, unbeknown, unbiased, unborn, unbroken, unbutton, uncanny, unceasing, uncertain, uncharted, unchecked, unclean, uncommitted, uncommon, unconscious, uncouth, uncover, undaunted, undecided, undeclared, undefended, undeniable, undesirable,undeterred, undeveloped, undo, undress, undying, unearthly, uneasy, uneaten, uneducated, unemployed, unexpected, unfailing, unfair, unfaithful, unfamiliar, unfeeling, unfit, unflappable, unfold, unforeseen, unforgettable, unfortunate, unfounded, unfriendly, unfurl, unfurnished, ungrateful, unguarded, unhappy, unhealthy, unheard, unhinge, unidentified, unimportant, uninhabitable, uninspired, uninterested, unjust, unkempt, unkind, unlike, unlimited, unload, unmanageable, unmentionable, unmistakable, unmoved, unnamed, unnatural, unnecessary, unobtrusive, unofficial, unorthodox, unpack, unplaced, unpleasant, unprintable, unprofessional, unprofitable, unprovoked, unquestionable, unravel, unreal, unreasonable, unrehearsed, unreliable, unrequited, unrest, unsuccessful, untidy, untie, untold, untrue, unusual, unveil, unwanted, unwell, unwilling, unwise, unwrap, unzip

IN

inability, inaccessible, inaccurate, inactive, inadequate, inanimate, inarticulate, inattentive, inaudible, incapable, incoherent, incombustible, incomparable, incompatible, incomplete, inconceivable, inconclusive, inconsiderate, inconsistent, inconvenient, incorrect, incredible, incurable, indecisive, indefinite, indelible, independent, indestructible, indignant, inedible, inept, infallible, infrequent, ingenious, ingratitude, inhuman, injustice, innocent, innumerate, insensitive, insufferable, insufficient, intolerable, invalid, invisible

IL

illegal, illegible, illegitimate, illiberal, illicit, illimitable, illiquid, illiterate, illogical

IM

imbalance, immaterial, immature, immeasurable, immobile, immoderate, immoral, immortal, immovable, immutable, impalpable, impartial, impassable, impassive, impatient, impenetrable, imperceptible, imperfect, imperishable, impermeable, impersonal, impertinent, impervious, impious, impolite, imponderable, important, impossible, impracticable, impractical, improbable, improper, improvident, imprudent, impure

IR

irrational, irreclaimable, irreconcilable, irrecoverable, irredeemable, irrefutable, irregular, irrelevant, irreligious, irremovable, irreparable, irreplaceable, irrepressible, irreproachable, irresistible, irresolute, irresolvable, irrespective, irresponsible, irretrievable, irreverent, irreversible, irrevocable

DIS

disable, disadvantage, disagree, disallow, disappear, disapprove, disarm, disarrange, disarray, disassociate, disbelieve, discharge, disclaim, discolour, discomfort, disconnect, discontent, discontinue, discourteous, discredit, disembark, disengage, disentangle, disfavour, dishonest, dishonour, disinfect, disinherit, dislike, dislodge, disloyal, dismount, disobey, disorder, disown, displace, displease, disprove, disqualify, disregard, dissatisfy, dissimilar, distrust

DE

deactivate, debrief, debug, decaffeinate, decamp, decapitate, decarbonise, decode, decolonise, decompose, decompress, deflate, deforest, defrock, defrost, defuse, degenerate, dehumanise, dehydrate, delouse, demerit, demilitarise, demist, deodorant, depopulate, derail, deregister, desegregate, dethrone, detour, devalue

NON

nonaligned, nonbeliever, noncombustible, noncommittal, noncompetitive, noncompulsory, noncontributory, nondescript, nondrinker, nondrip, nonexistent, nonfattening, nonferrous, non-fiction, nonflammable, nonfulfilment, nongovernmental, noninfectious, nonmalignant, nonmember, non-negotiable, non-nuclear, nonoperational, nonparticipation, nonpartisan, nonpayment, nonplaying, nonpractising, nonprofessional, non-profit-making, nonracial, nonrenewable, nonrepresentational, nonresident, nonreturnable, nonscientific, nonsegregated, nonsmoker, nonstandard, nonstarter, nonstick, nonstop, nontaxable, nontechnical, nontoxic, nontransferable, nonunion, nonverbal, nonviolent, nonvoter
(Many of these words can be written with a hyphen.)

Useful words lists

Other prefixes

A

aback, abide, ablaze, abloom, aboard, abound, afield, afloat, afoot, afore, afresh, aglitter, aglow, aground, alight, alike, alive, aloft, aloud, amass, amend, amid, amoral, anew, another, apace, apart, arise, around, ascribe, asexual, aside, asleep, astir, astray, astride, atone, atop, atypical, await, awake, awash, away

AB

abaft, abandon, abdicate, abduct, abjure, abnormal, abscond, abseil, absolve, abuse

AD

addition, adhere, adjacent, adjective, adjoin, adjudicate, adjust, administer, admire, admission, admixture, advance, advantage, advent, adventure, adverb, advert, advice, advise, advocate

AERO

aerobatics, aerobic, aerodrome, aerodynamic, aerofoil, aerogram, aerolite, aeronaut, aeronautics, aeroplane, aerosol, aerospace, aerostatics

AF

affable, affect, affection, affirm, affix, afflict, affluent, afforest, affray, affront

AL

almighty, almost, alone, already, also, although, altogether, always

ANTI

anti-aircraft, antiballistic missile, antibiotic, antibody, Antichrist, anticlerical, anticlimax, anticlockwise, anticoagulant, anticyclone, antidepressant, antidote, antifreeze, anti-hero, antihistamine, antiknock, anti-novel, antinuclear, antiparticle, anti-personnel, antiperspirant, antipope, anti-Semitic, antiseptic, antiserum, antisocial, antistatic, antitank, antithesis, antitoxin, antitrades, antitrust

AQUA

aqualung, aquaplane, aquarium, Aquarius, aquatic, aquatint

AUDI

audible, audience, audio, audiometer, audiotypist, audiovisual, audition, auditorium, auditory

AUTO

autobahn, autobiography, autocracy, autocrat, autocue, autograph, autogyro, automate, automatic, automation, automaton, automobile, automotive, autonomous, autonomy, autopilot, auto-suggestion

BI

biannual, biaxial, bicameral, bicentenary, biceps, bicolour, bicuspid, bicycle, biennial, bifid, bifocal, bifurcate, bikini, bilateral, bilingual, binary, binocular, binoculars, binomial, bipartite, biped, biplane, bipolar, bisect, bisexual, bivalve

CIRCUM

circumambient, circumambulate, circumcise, circumduct, circumference, circumfuse, circumnavigate, circumscribe, circumstance, circumvent

CO

coalition, co-author, coaxial, co-driver, coeducation (co-education), coefficient, coequal, coexist, coextend, cohabit, cohere, cohort, coincidence, collaborate, cooperate (co-operate), cooperation (co-operation), cooperative (co-operative), co-opt, coordinate (co-ordinate), coordinates, copartner, co-pilot, co-respondent, cosignatory (co-signatory), co-star, cotangent, co-worker, co-writer

CON

conciliate, conclave, conclude, concoct, concomitant, concord, concordance, concordat, concourse, concrete, concubine, concur, concurrence, concurrent, condense, condole, confab, confederacy, confer, conference, confide, confront, conglomerate, congregate, congregation, congress, congruent, conjoin, connect, consensus, conspire, construct, consult, contact, converge, convoy

CONTRA

contraception, contradict, contradictory, contraflow, contrariwise, contravene

CRED

credence, credential, credible, credulity, credulous

EX

exceed, excel, except, excess, exchange, exclaim, exclude, excrete, excursion, ex-directory, exempt, exhale, exhaust, exile, exit, exorcise, exoskeleton, expand, expatriate, expectorate, expel, expiration, expire, explode, export, expulsion, ex-serviceman, ex-servicewoman, extend, extension, exterior, external, extinguish, extract, extrude, exude

INTER

interact, interbreed, intercede, intercept, intercession, interchange, inter-city, intercom, intercommunicate, interconnect, intercontinental, intercourse, interdenominational, interdepartmental, interdependent, interface, interfuse, interject, interlace, interlard, interlay, interleaf, interline, interlink, interlock, interloper, interlude, intermarry, intermediary, intermingle, intermission, international, interplanetary, interplay, interpolate, interpose, interracial, interrelate, interscholastic, intersect, intersection, interspace, interstellar, interstice, intertwine, interval, intervene, interview, interwar, interweave

MICRO

micro, microbe, microbiology, microchemistry, microchip, microcircuit, microcomputer, microcosm, microdot, microelectronics, microfilm, microlight, micrometer, microminiaturisation, micron, micro-organism, microscope, microscopic, microsecond, microstructure, microsurgery

MIS

misadventure, misaligned, misalliance, misapply, misapprehend, misappropriate, misbegotten, misbehave, miscalculate, miscall, miscarry, miscast, misconception, misconduct, misconstrue, miscreant, misdeal, misdeed, misdemeanour, misdirect, misfire, misfit, misfortune, misgiving, misgovern, misguided, mishandle, mishap, mishear, mishit, misinform, misinterpret, misjudge, mislay, mislead, mismanage, mismatch, misnamed, misnomer, misplace, misprint, misquote, misread, misrepresent, misrule, misshapen, misspell, misspend, mistake, mistime, mistreat, mistrust, misunderstand, misuse

PORT

portable, portage, porter, portfolio, portmanteau

PRE

preamble, prearrange, precaution, precede, precedent, precognition, preconceive, precondition, precursor, predate, predecease, predecessor, predestination, predestine, predetermine, predict, predispose, pre-empt, prefabricate, preface, prefatory, prefigure, prefix, prehistoric, prejudge, preliminary, prelude, premarital, premature, premedication, premeditate, premenstrual, premolar, premonition, prenatal, preordain, prepacked, preparatory, prepare, prepay, prepossess, Pre-Raphaelite, prerecord, prerequisite, presage, preschool, prescience, prescribe, preset, presuppose, prevent, preview, previous, prewar

PRIM

primacy, prima donna, primal, primarily, primary, prime, primer, primeval, primitive, primogeniture, primordial

PRO

proactive, probability, probable, proceed, proclaim, proclivity, profess, progress, project, prologue, pronouncement, propel, propeller, prophesy, prophet, proponent, proposal, propose, propound, propulsion, prototype, protrude

SUB

subaltern, subaqua, subcommittee, subconscious, subcontract, subculture, subcutaneous, subdue, subeditor, subgroup, subheading, subhuman, submarine, submerge, submersible, submissive, subnormal, subordinate, subplot, subservient, subsoil, subsonic, substandard, subtitle, subway, subzero

SUPER

superabundant, superannuated, supercharge, supererogation, superglue, superhuman, superior, superlative, superman, supernumerary, superpower, superscript, supersonic, superstar, superstore, supertanker, supertax

SUS

suspect, suspend, suspension, suspicion

TELE

telecast, telecommunications, telegram, telegraph, telegraphy, telekinesis, telemeter, telepathy, telephone, telephony, telephoto lens, teleprinter, telesales, telescope, teletext, televise, television, telex

TRANS

transatlantic, transfer, transit, transmigrate, transmit, transport

TRI

triad, triangle, triangulate, triathlon, triceps, tricolour, tricycle, trident, triennial, trike, trilateral, trilogy, trinity, trio, triple, triplicate, tripod, triptych, trisect, trivet

RE

reactant, reactionary, reactivate, reactive, readjust, readmission, readmit, readopt, reaffirm, reafforest, realign, realignment, reallocate, reappear, reapply, reappoint, reappraisal, reappraise, rearrange, rearrest, reassemble, reassert, reassess, reawaken, rebate, rebirth, reborn, rebound, rebroadcast, rebuild, recall, recap, recapitulate, recapture, recharge, recheck, reclassify, recommence, recondition, reconnect, reconsider, reconstitute, reconstruct, reconvene, re-count, recoup, recover, recreate, recross, recycle, redecorate, redefine, redeploy, redesign, redevelop, redirect, rediscover, redistribute, redraft, redraw, re-echo, re-educate, re-elect, re-emerge, re-emphasise, re-employ, re-enact, re-enter, re-entry, re-equip, re-establish, re-examination, refashion, refreeze, refresh, refuel, refund, refurbish, refurnish, regain, rehash, rehouse, reimpose, reincarnate, reinsert, reinstate, reinsure, reinterpret, reintroduce, reissue, rejoin, relapse, relight, relive, reload, remake, remarry, remix, remodel, renegotiate, renumber, reoccupy, reoccurrence, reopen, reorder, reorganise, repaint, replace, replant, replenish, reproduce, reprogram, reread, reroute, rerun, reschedule, reseal, resettle, reshuffle, respray, restart, restate, restock, restructure, restyle, retake, retell, retrace, retract, retrain, retread, return, reunion, reuse, revalue, review, revisit, revive, rewire, reword, rework, rewrite

Hyphens and prefixes

Sometimes hyphens are used with certain prefixes. Hyphens can be used with the following prefixes:

ANTE

More often than not, this prefix is attached directly to the root word.

Words that use a hyphen include:

ante-bellum, ante-mortem, ante-post,

Words that do not use a hyphen include:

antecedent, antechamber, antechapel, antedate, antenatal, antependium

ANTI

Generally, it is only necessary to use a hyphen in order to make the meaning clear.

Words that use a hyphen include:

anti-aircraft, anti-apartheid, anti-personnel

BI

'bi' does not usually need a hyphen but it does in the following instances:

bi-weekly, bi-monthly, bi-yearly

BY

Words that use a hyphen include:

by-blow, by-election, by-product

Words that do not use a hyphen include:

bygone, bypass, byway, byword

CO

Most words with the prefix 'co' do not use a hyphen (or it is optional). There are two occasions when a hyphen can be used:

1 When the root or stem begins with 'o'.

co-operate, co-opt, co-ordinate

2 When the prefix means 'fellow' or 'shared'.

co-author, co-pilot, co-star

CROSS

This prefix tends to use a hyphen more often than not.

Words that usually use a hyphen include:

cross-Channel, cross-country, cross-current, cross-examine, cross-eyed, cross-fertilise, cross-infect, cross-legged, cross-ply, cross-pollinate, cross-purpose, cross-question, cross-reference, cross-section, cross-stitch

Words that do not use a hyphen include:

crossbar, crossbow, crosshatch, crossroads, crosstalk, crossways, crosswise, crossword

DE

A hyphen is only used when there might be confusion with a vowel at the beginning of the root word.

de-aerate, de-emphasise, de-escalate, de-ice

EX

The prefix 'ex' does not usually have a hyphen except in a few cases where the prefix means 'former' or 'exclusion'.

ex-captain, ex-chairman, ex-colleague, ex-directory, ex-servicewoman, ex-wife

EXTRA

Words that can use a hyphen include:

extra-curricular, extra-judicial, extra-marital, extra-sensory, extra-terrestrial

FAR

Words that use a hyphen include:

far-flung, far-off, far-out, far-reaching, far-sighted

IN

The following words sometimes use a hyphen:

in-built, in-depth, in-house, in-law, in-off, in-patient, in-tray

NEO

A hyphen is often used when the prefix means 'of a later or revived period'.

neo-classical, neo-colonial, neo-Nazi, neo-Victorian

Words that do not use a hyphen include:

Neolithic, neology, neomycin, neonatal, Neotropical

NON

Words that usually have a hyphen include:

non-Catholic, non-Christian, non-native, non-negotiable, non-nuclear, non-profit-making

OFF

Examples where a hyphen is used include:

off-centre, off-licence, off-line, off-load, off-peak, off-putting, off-season, off-stage, off-the-peg

Words where a hyphen is not used include:

offcut, offhand, offset, offshore, offside, offspring

ON

Words that use a hyphen include:

on-line, on-off, on-stage

Words that do not use a hyphen include:

oncoming, ongoing, onlooker, onrush, onset, onshore, onside, onslaught

OVER

Most words with this prefix do not use a hyphen. The following are words that can use a hyphen:

over-active, over-anxious, over-compensate, over-cooked, over-protective, over-sensitive, over-simplify, over-zealous

Words that do not use a hyphen include:

overact, overall, overarm, overcast, overcoat, overdo, overdress, overgrown, overhang, overhaul, overload, overpass, overreach, overrun, overseas, overshoot, oversleep, overspend, overstep, overtake, overthrow, overturn, overview, overwork, overwrought

PRE

A hyphen is used with root words that begin with 'e', such as:

pre-eminent, pre-empt, pre-emption, pre-emptive, pre-establish, pre-existence

Also it is used before words that begin with a capital letter, such as Pre-Raphaelite.

PRO

Rarely is 'pro' followed by a hyphen, except when it means 'in place of' or 'support', such as:

pro-chancellor, pro-Conservative, pro-Labour, pro-proctor

RE

A hyphen is used with 're' in the following cases:

1 When the root or stem begins with 'e'.

   re-edit, re-elect, re-embark, re-emerge, re-enact, re-engage, re-enter, re-establish

2 To avoid confusion with a similar word.

   re-cover (to cover again) and recover (to make a recovery), re-sign (to sign again) and resign (to give up)

SELF

This prefix nearly always has a hyphen, except for selfish and selfless.

SUB

A hyphen can sometimes be used when the prefix means 'lower' or 'a subsisiary part of'.

   sub-basement, sub-branch, sub-editor, sub-lieutenant, sub-plot, sub-post office

Otherwise a hyphen is generally not used.

VICE

Sometimes a hyphen can be used when the prefix means 'appointed substitute'.

   vice-admiral, vice-captain, vice-chairman, vice-president

A hyphen is not usually used, however, in the words viceregal and viceroy.

Spelling activities – prefixes

1 Ask the children to work out the meanings of words by providing them with the meaning of the prefix only; for example: If 're' means 'again', what might these words mean?

   recapture
   reword
   regain
   replay
   reconsider

2 Have a prefix race! Select a prefix that is familiar to the children and ask them to list as many words containing the prefix as they can think of. Combine the lists into a whole class reference and put on display for the children to add to over time.

3 Play 'Prefix lotto'. Make some grids with squares marked 1 to 6. Make some cards that will fit on the squares with prefixes on them that the children are familiar with. The players place a different prefix card on each square of the grid. Each player then throws a die. They look at the grid to see what prefix card is on that number square and the player has to write a word that contains that prefix. Score a point for each correct answer. Use dictionaries to check if necessary.

1 un	2 pre
3 dis	4 tri
5 mis	6 im

4 Have fun inventing new words with known prefixes; for example:

   megabottom = a very large bottom
   hydrochair = a chair that floats
   tridog = a three-legged dog
   aerocar = a car that travels through air
   autoreport = a report you write yourself

5 Play 'Prefix match'. Make up two sets of cards – one with prefixes and one with base words. The children place the cards face down in two separate piles. They take it in turns to turn over two cards – can they make a word? Score four points for each word made.

Suffixes

What are suffixes?

A suffix is a letter or group of letters added to the end of a base word. A suffix doesn't necessarily change the meaning of the base word but it makes the word fit with the way we wish to use it in a sentence.

For example:

> She had to complete the drawing.
> The drawing was comple**ly** finished.

Suffixes can change the part of speech of a word – thus a base word can generate verbs, nouns, adjectives or adverbs.

For example:
amuse**d**	verb
amuse**ment**	noun
amus**ing**	adjective
amusing**ly**	adverb

Suffixes include the plural endings of base words. Most words form the plural by simply adding 's', but there are many other rules that apply to plurals and these are dealt with in detail in Chapter 8.

Suffixes can also be used to make comparatives.
For example: small   small**er** small**est**

SUFFIX RULES

1   General rule
The spelling of a suffix never changes (except when adding 'full'), but the spelling of the base word sometimes does.
For example: beauty   beautiful

2   The doubling rule
a   Words of one syllable
When a word of one syllable ends in a short vowel followed by a single consonant, the last consonant is doubled when adding a suffix beginning with a vowel, such as 'ed' and 'ing'.
For example: (For word list see page 68.)
hop	ho**pp**ed	ho**pp**ing
plan	pla**nn**ed	pla**nn**ing

Exception: When the final consonant is 'x' you do not doubleit.
For example:
tax	taxed	taxing
vex	vexed	vexing

When a word ends in a short vowel followed by TWO consonants, the last consonant is NOT doubled.

For example:
test	tested	testing
help	helped	helping

When the suffix begins with a consonant, such as 'ness' and 'ly', the final consonant of the word is NOT doubled.
For example:
wet	wetness
hot	hotly

b   Words of more than one syllable
If the stress is on the first (or earlier) syllable, then the consonant is not doubled before adding the suffix.
For example:
ballot	balloted	balloting
focus	focused	focusing

If the stress is on the last syllable, then the consonant IS doubled before adding the suffix.
For example: (For word list see page 68.)
admit	admitted	admitting
equip	equipped	equipping

Almost invariably, if a word ends with 'l', irrespective of where the stress falls, the 'l' is doubled before adding a suffix beginning with a vowel. For example:
cancel	cancelled	cancelling
enrol	enrolled	enrolling

As with single syllable words, the final consonant is not doubled if the suffix begins with a consonant.
For example:
commit	commitment
level	levelness

3   Silent or magic 'e' words
If a suffix begins with a vowel, the general rule is to drop the 'e' before adding the ending.
For example:
fine	fined
hide	hiding
argue	arguable
conspire	conspiracy
collapse	collapsible
analyse	analysis

Note: this final 'e' was sounded in Old and Middle English

Exceptions: see page 63.

When a word ends in 'ge' or 'ce', keep the 'e' before adding 'able' or 'ous'. This is to keep the consonant sounding soft.
For example:
change   changeable
(For exceptions see page 59.)

If the suffix begins with a consonant, the silent 'e' is usually retained.
For example:
care + full = careful
              (one 'l' in the suffix is dropped)
bare + ly = barely
arrange + ment = arrangement

Exceptions:
argue + ment = argument
due + ly = duly
true + ly = truly
whole + ly = wholly

In words that end in 'ie', the 'ie' changes to 'y' before adding 'ing'.
For example:
tie   tying

4 Words that end in 'a', 'i', 'o' and 'u'
When words end in 'a', 'i', 'o' or 'u', they are usually unaffected by added a suffix.
For example:
echo   echoed   echoing
taxi   taxied   taxiing

5 Words that end in 'y'
If there is a consonant before the 'y', change the 'y' to 'i' before adding the suffix.
For example: (For word list see page 69.)
easy   easier   easiest   easily
carry carrier carries   carried carriage

But note: the 'y' is kept before adding 'ing' to avoid having two 'i's together; so carry, carrying.

If there is a vowel before the 'y', just add the suffix.
For example:
employ   employed   employing   employment
play   played   playing   playful

6 Adding 'full'
When the word 'full' is added to another word, one 'l' is always dropped.
For example: (For word list see page 62.)
dread + full = dreadful
peace + full = peaceful

Most words retain the final 'e' before adding 'ful', except awe – awful.

If there is a consonant before the 'y', change the 'y' to 'i' before adding the suffix – beauty, beautiful; mercy, merciful; pity, pitiful

When 'ly' is added to words ending in 'ful', it forms 'fully' at the end; thus: dreadfully and peacefully.

7 Adding 'y' (to form adjectives or adverbs)
Most words just add the 'y', but the doubling and drop 'e' rules also apply.
For example:
cloud + y = cloudy
fun + y = funny
stripe + y = stripy

(For word list see page 67.)

8 Adding 'ly'
If a word ends in 'l', just add the 'ly'.
For example: (For word list see page 64.)
cool + ly = coolly
formal + ly = formally
For most other words, simply add 'ly'. But note there are exceptions for words that end in 'y', 'ic', 'ble' and 'ple'.
For example:
complete + ly = completely
vigorous + ly = vigorously

But:
a If the word ends in 'y', the 'y' changes to 'i' before adding 'ly.'
For example:
busy + ly = busily
necessary + ly = necessarily

b If a word ends in 'ic', you normally add 'ally', not just 'ly'.
For example:
analytic + ally = analytically
tragic + ally = tragically

But 'public' becomes 'publicly'.

c If a word ends in 'ble', the ending becomes 'bly'.
For example:
humble + ly = humbly
capable + ly = capably

d If a word ends in 'ple', the ending becomes 'ply'.
For example:
ample + ly = amply
simple + ly = simply

9 When 'k' is added to a word ending in 'c'
A word ending in 'c' will usually add 'k before a suffix that begins with 'e', 'i' or 'y'. This is to keep the hard sound of the 'c'.
For example:

| picnic | picnicked | picnicking | picnicker |
| frolic | frolicked | frolicking | frolicky |

10 When vowels are dropped or changed in words after adding a suffix
Sometimes a letter will drop out or change in the base word when a suffix is added.

a In words ending in 'our', you drop the 'u' when adding 'ous'.
For example:
humour + ous = humorous
rigour + ous = rigorous

The 'u' is also dropped before some other suffixes, such as:
glamour + ise = glamorise
humour + ist = humorist
rigour + ism = rigorism
rigour + ist = rigorist

b Words ending in 'er' and 'or' sometimes drop the 'e' or 'o' before the suffix.
For example:
hunger + y = hungry
disaster + ous = disastrous
enter + ance = entrance
hinder + ance = hindrance

Exceptions: adulteress, adulterous, boisterous, murderess, murderous, slanderous

c Words ending in 'nounce' sometimes drop the 'o' before the suffix.
For example:
announce + iate = annunciate
pronounce + iation = pronunciation

d Words that end in 'claim' sometimes drop the 'i' before the suffix.
For example:
exclaim + 'ation' = exclamation
proclaim + 'ation' = proclamation

11 With words that end in 'f', the 'f' changes to 'v' before a vowel suffix is added.
For example:
grief + ous = grievous
mischief + ous = mischievous
thief + ing = thieving
relief + ed = relieved

12 Comparatives
a Just add 'er' for the comparative and 'est' for the superlative.
For example:

| clean | cleaner | cleanest |
| long | longer | longest |

But if the word ends in 'e', just add 'r' for the comparative and 'st' for the superlative.
For example:

| large | larger | largest |
| wise | wiser | wisest |

b If a word ends in 'y' which is preceded by a consonant, change the 'y' into 'i' before adding 'er' and 'est'.
For example:

| busy | busier | busiest |
| merry | merrier | merriest |

c The same rules for doubling (see page 48) when adding other suffixes apply to comparatives.
Thus:
You would double the last letter in:

big	bigger	biggest
flat	flatter	flattest
red	redder	reddest

Choosing the right suffix

Some word endings sound very alike and this can cause problems with spelling so it can help to know a few generalised rules:

'ABLE' OR 'IBLE'?

There is no simple, overriding rule to sort out which words end in 'able' or 'ible', but 'able' is more common. 'able' is usually the correct suffix when added to a word that is not altered before it is added; for example:

adapt	adaptable
laugh	laughable
pass	passable
suit	suitable

Other things to keep in mind include:

a Nouns that end in 'ation' become 'able' when forming an adjective. For example:

consideration	considerable
conservation	conservable
duration	durable
navigation	navigable
translation	translatable

b Verbs that end in 'ate' become 'able' when forming an adjective. For example:

irritate	irritable
rate	rateable (or ratable)
separate	separable

c 'ible' is usual if preceded by the letter 's'. For example:

accessible	possible
collapsible	sensible
divisible	visible

d Nouns that end in 'ion' usually become 'ible' when forming related words. For example:

audition	audible
combustion	combustible

e 'ible' is usually added to word bases that are not complete words. For example:
audible
edible
indelible

f In both 'able' and 'ible' endings, you usually drop the 'e' in silent 'e' words before adding the suffix. For example:

adore	adorable
move	movable
response	responsible
sense	sensible

But note that words with a soft 'c' or 'g' retain the final 'e' before adding 'able' to keep the sound soft. For example:

charge	chargeable
manage	manageable
notice	noticeable
service	serviceable

And note that the following words can also retain the 'e' (but it is dropped from the base word when adding 'ing'):

blameable	nameable
giveable	saleable
hireable	sizeable
likeable	

g The same doubling rules (see page 48) apply to words that have an 'able' or an 'ible' suffix; thus:

commit	committed	committing	committable
regret	regretted	regretting	regrettable

But if the same base word varies its stress from the last syllable with some suffixes, this affects whether the final consonant is doubled, thus:

prefer	preferred	preferring	preferable
refer	referred	referring	referable
transfer	transferred	transferring	transferable

Note: when a 'ble' ending is changed to 'bly', 'able' becomes simply 'ably' and 'ible' becomes 'ibly'. For example:

abominable	abominably
credible	credibly

How can you remember all these rules for 'able' and 'ible' endings?

One way is to stress the ending each time you write the word. For example:

irrit**able**	(Learn it as: irrit **able**)
horr**ible**	(Learn it as: horr **ible**)

Another way is to make up mnemonics of words and group them together. Remember – the sillier they are the better! For example:

He is acceptable, adaptable, adorable, amiable, capable, desirable, hospitable, impeccable, indispensable, knowledgeable, likeable, lovable, peaceable, pleasurable, reliable, suitable, tolerable and unmistakably marriageable!

It may also be helpful to be aware that words ending in 'able' usually have their root in the Latin ending 'abilis' or the Old French 'able', while words ending in 'ible' have their root in the Latin ending 'ibilis'.

(For word lists see page 59.)

'ARY', 'ERY', 'ORY' OR 'URY'?

Pronunciation is sometimes a good test of the differences between these spellings.
'ary' and 'ory' tend to be adjective endings.
'ery' and 'ury' are noun endings.

imaginary	advisory
complimentary	satisfactory
veterinary	respiratory

'ery' is usually added to a base word, such as:

fish	fishery
green	greenery
hatch	hatchery
machine	machinery
trick	trickery

The few words that end in 'ury' include:
augury, century, fury, injury, jury, luxury, mercury, penury, perjury, treasury, usury.

Mnemonics can help you remember tricky words with these endings, such as:

station**ery**	and	station**ary**
comp**le**mentary	and	comp**li**mentary
access**ary**	and	access**ory**

For example:
You are station**a**ry at the st**a**tion where you st**a**nd.
Envelopes are station**e**ry.
An **o**rnament is an access**o**ry.
An access**a**ry is someone who **a**ids and **a**bets.
His pr**ai**se and adm**i**ration were compl**i**mentary.
Sh**e** had the compl**e**mentary s**e**t.

(For word lists see page 62.)

'TION', 'SION', 'SSION', 'CIAN', 'TIAN' OR 'XION'?

Words with these endings all have much the same 'shun' pronunciation. However, there are some general guidelines that can help decide which ending to use. One thing they have in common is that, for the most part, they are all nouns.

tion
The majority of words with a 'shun' sound end in 'tion'. Verbs that end in 't', 'te' or 'fy' normally have 'tion' in the noun form. For example:

inflect	inflection
rotate	rotation
electrify	electrification

sion
Words with this ending are often formed from verbs ending in 'd', 'de', 'se' or sometimes 't'. For example:

comprehend	comprehension
collide	collision
infuse	infusion
subvert	subversion

ssion
Nouns with this ending usually come from verbs that end in 'ss'. They can also come from verbs ending in 'mit' (derived from the Latin verb *mittere*), 'cede' or 'ceed'. For example:

confess	confession
admit	admission
concede	concession
preceed	procession

cian
This suffix indicates a person skilled at something. There are very few words that have this ending and are pronounced 'shun'. They include:
beautician
electrician
magician
politician

xion
Very few words have this ending. They include:
deflexion (or deflection)
inflexion (or inflection)
genuflexion (or genuflection)

tian
A few words have this ending, such as:
Dalmatian
Martian

(For word lists see pages 66–67.)

'ANT' OR 'ENT'? / 'ANCE' OR 'ENCE'?

Unfortunately there are few guidelines for these endings. It is difficult to hear any difference between the two endings because the voice drops at the end of the word. However, the following can help:

1   Words that end in 'ent' generally take the suffix 'ence' and those ending in 'ant' become 'ance'.

2   'ant' and 'ance' occur after a hard 'c' or 'g'. For example:
significant   significance
arrogant   arrogance

3   'ent' and 'ence' occur after a soft 'c' or 'g'. For example:
magnificent   magnificence
diligent   diligence

Otherwise, mnemonics can be used to help you remember words that give you particular difficulties. For example:

1   Make up lists of 'ant' words. Draw ants (the insects) to look like their meaning (see below).

2   Find smaller words within the words. For example:
ab**sent**
atten**dance**
inno**cent**
pun**gent**

3   Make up rhymes or sentences. For example:

It becomes appa**rent** when you haven't paid the **rent**.
Some **men** made the orna**men**t.
Parents have children ap**parent**ly!
The **gent** was very indi**gent**.
We **sent** the pre**sent**.
The campers are con**tent** in their **tent**.
The ty**rant rant**ed and raved.
The emi**grant** was **grant**ed permission to leave.

(For word lists see pages 60–61.)

giant

slant

migrant

plant

transplant

jubilant

buoyant

'ACLE', 'ICAL' OR 'ICLE'?

'ical' can be separated from the others because it is an adjective ending, not a noun. For example:

> comical
> identical
> musical

'icle' and 'acle' are both noun endings. Pronunciation is usually a good guide to which one to use:

If the ending is pronounced 'uhcul', the spelling is usually 'acle'. For example:

> barnacle
> obstacle
> tentacle

If the ending is pronounced 'ickul', the spelling is normally 'icle'. For example:

> article
> icicle
> vehicle

(For word lists see page 59.)

'AR', 'ER', 'OR', 'RE' OR 'OUR'?

Pronunciation can sometimes give a fairly clear indication of which to use, but not always!

'ar' as a noun ending is fairly rare, so you could just learn the few examples:

altar	collar
beggar	familiar
burglar	grammar
calendar	scholar
caterpillar	tsar (or czar)
cellar	vicar

But as an adjective ending, 'ar' is quite common. For example:

familiar	lumbar
jocular	modular
lunar	vehicular

'er' sometimes indicates an Old English word and an early or basic occupation. For example:

baker	butcher
farmer	gardener
gaoler	lender
maker	printer
teacher	worker

'er' is also very common as a comparative adjective. For example:

better	bigger
faster	hotter
smaller	taller

Words with a soft 'c' or 'g' will need an 'er' ending to keep the 'c' or 'g' soft. For example:

grocer	manager
officer	ranger

'er' is used in words for relations, such as:

mother	father
sister	brother
daughter	

'or' indicates a more modern activity or profession. For example:

author	doctor
professor	solicitor
surveyor	vendor

'or' is used when the base word ends in 'ate', 'ct', 'it' or 'ession'. For example:

operate	operator
collect	collector
edit	editor
succession	successor

Some words can be spelled with either an 'er' or an 'or' ending, such as:

> conjuror / conjurer
> advisor / adviser
> conveyor / conveyer
> castor / caster
> adaptor / adapter

're' – most words ending in a consonant followed by 're' are nouns. For example:

acre	calibre
centre	metre
ochre	theatre

'our' – there are no guidelines to help you decide when to use 'our' endings, so it is a matter of learning these words as you use them. Examples include:

behaviour	honour
hour	labour
neighbour	savour

(For word lists see page 61.)

'EOUS', 'IOUS' OR 'OUS'?

These suffixes mean 'full of' or 'like'. For example: furious means full of fury.

'ous' is used after a complete word that ends in a consonant. For example:

danger	dangerous
mountain	mountainous

If the base word ends in a silent 'e', the 'e' is dropped before adding 'ous'. For example:

grieve	grievous
nerve	nervous
rapture	rapturous
ridicule	ridiculous

In words with a soft 'c' or 'g' an 'i' is substituted for the 'e' to keep the letters soft. For example:

grace	gracious
space	spacious

But note: advantag**e**ous, courag**e**ous, gorg**e**ous and outrag**e**ous.

Nouns that end in 'f' change to 'v' before the ending. For example:

grief	grievous
mischief	mischievous

Words or stems ending in 'our' drop the 'u' before adding 'ous'. For example:

glamour	glamorous
humour	humorous
rigour	rigorous
vigour	vigorous

'ous' is also used after words or stems ending in 'u'. For example:

ambiguous	conspicuous
deciduous	impetuous
sensuous	vacuous

When 'ous' is added to words that end in 'y', either:
'y' becomes 'i' before adding 'ous', or
'y' becomes 'e' before adding 'ous'.
For example:

fury	fur**ious**
glory	glor**ious**
industry	industr**ious**
vary	var**ious**
beauty	beaut**eous**
courtesy	court**eous**
pity	pit**eous**
plenty	plent**eous**

Some 'eous' words are easy to distinguish because the 'e' makes a clearly pronounced 'ee' sound. For example:

aqueous	bounteous
courteous	cutaneous

hideous	miscellaneous
nauseous	simultaneous
spontaneous	

Unfortunately, some 'ious' words are also pronounced like the 'e' in 'eous':

bilious	ceremonious
curious	delirious
notorious	previous
sanctimonious	serious

(For word lists see pages 64–65.)

'AL', 'EL' OR 'LE'?

In words with a soft 'c' or 'g' before the final 'ul' sound, the ending will usually be 'el'. For example: parcel and angel.

Words with a hard 'c' before the final 'ul' sound use either 'le' or 'al'. The choice between a 'cle' or a 'cal' ending depends on the way the word is used. 'cle' words are nouns and 'cal' words are adjectives. For example:

classical	circle
critical	cubicle
magical	icicle
musical	miracle
physical	vehicle

It is also helpful to note that 'mle', 'nle', 'rle', 'vle' and 'wle' endings are not used in English words. So the 'ul' sound after 'm', 'n', 'r', 'v' and 'w' can only be made by 'el' or 'al'.

Some 'el' words follow no specific guidelines, such as:

chapel	cruel
expel	fuel
label	model
parallel	vessel

There are no reliable guidelines for working out which words will be 'al' so it is best to learn these words as you use them. They include:

approval	hospital
material	metal
proposal	rehearsal
signal	special

If you are unsure of which ending to use, it is always helpful to write the word down, and, if it looks wrong, try another ending. If you still cannot tell whether it looks right, use a dictionary to check. It is easy to look up words where you are unsure of the ending because you already have the beginning of the word.

(For word list see pages 60.)

CHANGING PARTS OF SPEECH BY USING SUFFIXES

Suffixes can be used to change parts of speech For example:

1 To change a noun to a verb, add 'ise' ('ize').

For example:

anaesthesia	anaesthetise (ize)
drama	dramatise (ize)
economy	economise (ize)
terror	terrorise (ize)

2 To change a verb to a noun, add 'tion', 'ion', 'sion', 'ssion' or 'ation'.

For example:

reject	rejection
compile	compilation
infuse	infusion
confess	confession

Or, add 'al', 'se', 'ment', 'iture' or 'ance'.

For example:

refuse	refusal
expend	expense
govern	government
persevere	perseverance

Or, add 'er', 'or', 'ant' or 'ent'.

For example:

audit	auditor
expedite	expedient
labour	labourer
supply	supplier

3 To change a noun to an adjective, add 'ful', 'less', 'ious', 'eous', 'ous' or 'y'

For example:

hope	hopeful
end	endless
beauty	beauteous
ambition	ambitious
chill	chilly

Or, add 'al', 'ic', 'ish', 'an', 'ary' or 'ed'.

For example:

nature	natural
fever	feverish
America	American
psychosis	psychotic
imagination	imaginary
colour	coloured

4 To change an adjective to a noun, add 'ness', 'ity', 'ce' or 'cy'.

For example:

happy	happiness
romantic	romance
loquacious	loquacity
fragrant	fragrance

5 To change an adjective to a verb, add 'ise' ('ize'), 'en' or 'fy'.

For example:

fertile	fertilise (ize)
thick	thicken
liquid	liquefy
solid	solidify

6 To change a verb to an adjective, add 'able', 'ible' or 'ive'.

For example:

reverse	reversible
manage	manageable
support	supportive

7 To change an adjective to an adverb, add 'ly'.

For example:

happy	happily
angry	angrily

8 To change a noun to an adverb, add 'wise'.

For example:

like	likewise
length	lengthwise

Common suffixes

Note: words in italics are of Greek origin. Others are Latin or as marked.

Suffix	Meaning	Examples
able, ably	able to, capable of being	inflatable, lovable, profitable
ac, iac	pertaining to	hypochondriac, cardiac
acy	state or quality of being	democracy, intricacy, delicacy
age	belonging to, related to	postage, acreage, mileage, marriage
agia, algia	pain	neuralgia
al	pertaining to, act of, like	environmental, infinitesimal
an, ant, ent	one who is	Puritan, blatant, strident, confident
ance	act of, state of being	conveyance, abeyance
ar	relating to, like	polar, singular
ary	a place for, like, belonging	infirmary, legendary hereditary
ate	having, cause	alienate, incarnate
ation, ition	the act of, result of	alteration, partition
cide, cidal	killer, power to kill	insecticide, suicidal
cracy crat, cracy	government, rule	democrat, bureaucracy
dom (OE)	jurisdiction, realm, quality of being	kingdom, earldom, wisdom, freedom
en (OE)	to become	blacken, weaken
ence	act, fact, state, quality	conference, potence excellence
ency	state of being	dependency
er (OE)	one who, comparative	gaoler, interpreter, better
ery, ry (& OF)	a place to/for occupation of	dentistry, tannery, vinery
escence	becoming	adolescence
ful (OE)	full of	painful, mouthful

Suffix	Meaning	Examples
fy	to make, cause to be	magnify, horrify
genesis genesis	creation, formation	parthenogenesis
genic (E)	suitable	photogenic
gram	record/write	cardiogram
graph	write	telegraph, autograph
graphy	process/ method of writing	calligraphy, photography
hood (OE)	state, quality, group of	adulthood, childhood
ia, y	act, state of	euphoria, dyslexia, polity
ian	belonging to, relating to	vegetarian, plebeian
iatrics	treatment of a disease	paediatrics
iatry	healing	psychiatry
ible	able to be	edible, legible, visible
ic, ic	pertaining to	endemic, politic
ical	pertaining to	angelical, political
il, ile	having to do with	civil, docile
ine (F)	like, feminine	crystalline, concubine, feminine
ion	the act or result of, one who	opinion, companion, union, champion
ise, ize	to make, to give	sanitise, verbalise
ish (OE)	of, like	boyish, childish
isk, iscus	little	asterisk
ism, ism	the belief in, profession of	journalism, baptism
ist, ist	a person who does, one who believes in	conversationalist, baptist
itis	inflammation	iritis, meningitis
itude (tude)	state of being	aptitude

Suffix	Meaning	Examples
ity	state, character, condition	stability, sanctity, obesity
ium	the act of	colloquium
ive	one who, that which is	elusive, pensive, persuasive
less (OE)	without, lacking	ruthless, shameless, tireless, thoughtless
like (ME)	characteristic of, suitable for	childlike, workmanlike
lite, lith	stone	stalactite, monolith
logue	manner of speaking	dialogue, monologue
logy	science or study of	geology, biology
ly (OE)	specified manner, extent	hourly, sharply, suitably
lysis	loosening	analysis
m, ma, me	result of	theorem, dogma, theme
mania	madness for	cleptomania
ment, mentum	result, or means of an act	impediment, momentum
meter	measure	barometer
ness (OE)	state, quality of being	happiness, sadness
oid, oid	resembling, like, shaped	cuboid, humanoid
oma	tumour	melanoma
or	person or thing who	actor, creator
orama	view	panorama
ory	relating to, thing which, place where	laboratory, factory, ambulatory
osis, osis	abnormal condition	myxomatosis, halitosis

Suffix	Meaning	Examples
pathy	feeling, disease	apathy, osteopathy
phobia	fear of	claustrophobia
phone	sound	telephone
phor	that which carries	metaphor
phoria	production	euphoria
phorous	producing	phosphorous
poly	sale, selling	monopoly
scope	instrument for visual examination	telescope, microscope, endoscope
ship (OE)	quality, condition, state of	friendship, fellowship, comradeship
sis	process	analysis
some (OE)	like, tending to be	loathsome, tiresome
sphere	globe, ball	hemisphere
therapy	to nurse, care for	aromatherapy
tic	pertaining to	automatic
tion, sion	act, process of, result of	locomotion, pension, exhaustion
tude (& F)	state of being	attitude, aptitude
ure (& F)	state, act of	censure, tenure
vorous, vore	eating, feeding on	carnivorous, herbivore
wise (OE)	direction, manner, in regard to	anticlockwise, streetwise
y, y (& OE)	quality, diminutive, state	sandy, shiny, doggy, jealousy

Useful words lists

Note: in the following words lists, many of the words have alternative spellings that are also correct.

'ABLE'

abominable, acceptable, actionable, adaptable, admirable, admittable, adorable, advisable, agreeable, alienable, amenable, amiable, appreciable, arguable, assessable, atonable, available, avoidable, bearable, believable, blameable, bribable, bridgeable, calculable, capable, changeable, chargeable, conceivable, conferrable, considerable, consolable, contractable, creatable, curable, datable, debatable, deferrable, definable, demonstrable, desirable, despicable, durable, dutiable, dyable, eatable, educable, endorsable, equable, excisable, excitable, excusable, expendable, forseeable, forgettable, forgivable, giveable, hireable, hospitable, immovable, immutable, impassable, impeccable, imperturbable, implacable, impressionable, indefatigable, indescribable, indispensable, indubitable, inescapable, inevitable, inferable, inflammable, inflatable, inimitable, insufferable, irreconcilable, irreplaceable, irritable, justifiable, knowledgeable, laughable, likeable, lovable, machinable, malleable, manageable, manoeuvrable, marriageable, measurable, movable, noticeable, objectionable, obtainable, operable, palatable, passable, payable, peaceable, penetrable, perishable, permeable, pleasurable, practicable, preferable, pronounceable, provable, rateable, readable, reconcilable, rectifiable, referable, regrettable, reliable, removable, reputable, retractable, saleable, serviceable, sizeable, solvable, storable, tolerable, traceable, tradable, undeniable, unexceptionable, unmistakable, unshakeable, usable, variable, veritable, washable, workable

Most words drop the silent 'e' before adding 'able'. But several groups of words are exceptions:

1. Words with a soft 'c' or 'g':
   bridgeable, changeable, chargeable, irreplaceable, knowledgeable, manageable, marriageable, noticeable, peaceable, pronounceable, serviceable, traceable

2. blameable, giveable, hireable, likeable, nameable, saleable, sizeable

'IBLE'

accessible, admissible, audible, avertible, collapsible, combustible, compatible, comprehensible, contemptible, convertible, corruptible, credible, defensible, destructible, digestible, discernible, divisible, edible, eligible, exhaustible, expressible, extendible, extensible, fallible, feasible, flexible, forcible, fusible, gullible, inaccessible, inaudible, incorrigible, incorruptible, incredible, indelible, indigestible, infallible, intangible, intelligible, invincible, irascible, irrepressible, irresistible, legible, negligible, ostensible, perceptible, permissible, plausible, possible, repressible, reproducible, resistible, responsible, reversible, sensible, susceptible, tangible, terrible, visible

Words that drop the 'e' before adding 'ible' include: collapsible, defensible, forcible, fusible, reducible, reproducible, responsible, reversible, sensible.

'ACLE'

barnacle, coracle, debacle, manacle, miracle, obstacle, oracle, pinnacle, receptacle, spectacle, tabernacle, tentacle

'ICAL'

aeronautical, alphabetical, anatomical, archaeological, astronomical, asymmetrical, biblical, biographical, biological, chronological, comical, conical, critical, cubical, cyclical, cylindrical, diagrammatical, farcical, geographical, geological, grammatical, helical, historical, hysterical, identical, impractical, logical, mathematical, mechanical, medical, methodical, musical, mystical, mythical, nautical, ornithological, paradoxical, pharmaceutical, phonological, physical, psychological, quizzical, radical, seismological, spherical, technical, technological, tropical, typical, vertical, whimsical

'ICLE'

article, auricle, chicle, chronicle, clavicle, conventicle, cubicle, cuticle, epicuticle, follicle, icicle, ossicle, panicle, particle, pedicle, radicle, reticle, testicle, vehicle, ventricle, vesicle

'AL'

aboriginal, accidental, accusal, acquittal, additional, adjectival, agricultural, anecdotal, appraisal, approval, arousal, arrival, autumnal, bacterial, baptismal, basal, behavioural, betrayal, betrothal, bridal, brutal, burial, centrifugal, classical, clausal, clerical, clinical, coastal, coeducational, comical, committal, communal, compartmental, conditional, confessional, confrontational, congregational, constitutional, continental, continual, critical, cultural, cynical, deferral, deflectional, departmental, deposal, developmental, diabolical, digital, dimensional, directional, dismissal, dispersal, disposal, dramatical, educational, electrical, elemental, elliptical, emotional, ethical, exceptional, experimental, fanatical, fictional, fractional, frontal, functional, geometrical, gestural, global, governmental, graphical, herbal, heretical, heroical, historical, homicidal, hormonal, illogical, institutional, instructional, instrumental, intentional, ironical, judgmental, lineal, logical, lyrical, magical, marginal, mathematical, mayoral, medicinal, modal, monsoonal, musical, mystical, national, natural, navigational, nodal, notional, observational, oppositional, optical, optional, orbital, oriental, original, ornamental, parental, pastoral, periodical, perusal, phenomenal, philosophical, phrasal, physical, pictural, pivotal, poetical, portrayal, postal, professional, proportional, proposal, rational, recital, referral, refusal, regional, rehearsal, remittal, removal, renewal, rental, retrieval, revival, seasonal, sensational, spinal, spiral, suicidal, temperamental, tidal, tonal, topical, tribal, urinal, zonal

'ANCE'

abundance, advance, alliance, ambiance, appearance, arrogance, askance, assonance, attendance, balance, chance, cognizance, countenance, dance, defiance, dissonance, distance, disturbance, dominance, elegance, entrance, extravagance, exuberance, finance, France, glance, grievance, guidance, hesitance, instance, insurance, irrelevance, lance, maintenance, nuisance, obeisance, ordinance, ordnance, outdistance, performance, permeance, perseverance, pittance, prance, precipitance, predominance, preponderance, protuberance, pursuance, purveyance, radiance, reassurance, reconnaissance, reinsurance, reliance, reluctance, remembrance, renaissance, repugnance, resemblance, resistance, resonance, riddance, romance, séance, semblance, stance, substance, sufferance, superabundance, surveillance, trance, valance, variance

'ENCE'

absence, beneficence, cadence, competence, consequence, consistence, correspondence, credence, decadence, defence, difference, emergence, equivalence, essence, evidence, excellence, existence, expedience, experience, fence, flatulence, hence, imminence, impotence, impudence, inadvertence, indolence, insolence, licence, magnificence, obedience, occurrence, offence, omnipotence, omnipresence, omniscience, opulence, pence, penitence, permanence, persistence, phosphorescence, potence, precedence, pre-eminence, preference, prescience, presence, pretence, providence, prudence, quiescence, quintessence, recurrence, redolence, reference, reminiscence, renascence, residence, resilience, resplendence, resurgence, reverence, sapience, science, sentence, sequence, silence, spence, subsequence, subservience, succulence, thence, valence, whence

'ENSE'

condense, commonsense, dense, dispense, expense, frankincense, immense, incense, intense, license, nonsense, prepense, recompense, recondense, sense, suspense, tense

'ANT'

abundant, adamant, adjutant, arrogant, ascendant, assonant, attendant, blatant, buoyant, claimant, cognizant, constant, currant, dependant, descendant, dissonant, distant, dominant, elegant, elephant, emigrant, extant, extravagant, exuberant, flagrant, flippant, fondant, fragrant, gallant, giant, hesitant, important, instant, irrelevant, itinerant, jubilant, mendicant, militant, pant, peasant, pedant, penchant, pendant, pheasant, plant, pleasant, poignant, precipitant, predominant, pregnant, propellant, protestant, protuberant, pursuant, rampant, rant, recalcitrant, redundant, refrigerant, relevant, reluctant, repugnant, resonant, restaurant, resultant, reverberant, ruminant, significant, slant, stagnant, superabundant, supplicant, sycophant, transplant, trenchant, truant, tyrant, vagrant, valiant, variant, verdant, vibrant

'ENT'

absent, abstinent, accent, advent, agent, ardent, ascent, belligerent, beneficient, benevolent, bent, cadent, cement, cent, client, coefficient, coherent, competent, consequent, consistent, content, convent, corespondent, current, decadent, decent, deficient, delinquent, dent, dependent, deterrent, different, diffident, diligent, dissident, efficient, emergent, eminent, equivalent, event, evident, excellent, expedient, extent, flatulent, fluent, fluorescent, frequent, gent, imminent, impotent, impudent, inadvertent, incandescent, incipient, incumbent, indent, independent, indigent, inefficient, insipient, insolent, intent, invent, lament, latent, lenient, lent, lucent, magnificent, moment, munificent, nascent, obedient, occident, omnipotent, omnipresent, omniscient, orient, parent, patent, patient, pendent, penitent, percipient, permanent, phosphorescent, portent, potent, precedent, pre-eminent, prescient, present, president, proficient, propellent, proponent, provident, prudent, prurient, pungent, putrescent, quiescent, quotient, recent, recipient, recurrent, redolent, regent, relent, reminiscent, renascent, rent, repellent, repent, resilient, resplendent, respondent, resurgent, reticent, reverent, rodent, salient, sapient, scent, sent, sentient, silent, spent, strident, stringent, subsequent, subservient, succulent, superintendent, talent, tangent, tent, transient, transparent, trident, truculent, turbulent, undercurrent, urgent, vent, went

'AR'

afar, ajar, altar, angular, annular, articular, beggar, binocular, budgerigar, burglar, bursar, calendar, car, caterpillar, caviar, cedar, cellar, char, Cheddar, cigar, circular, collar, cougar, curricular, czar, dissimilar, dollar, exemplar, familiar, far, fibular, fulmar, funicular, grammar, granular, guitar, hangar, hussar, insular, irregular, isobar, jaguar, jocular, jugular, liar, lumbar, lunar, mar, modular, molar, molecular, mortar, muscular, nebular, nodular, ocular, particular, peculiar, pedlar, peninsular, pillar, polar, poplar, popular, premolar, pulsar, radar, rectangular, registrar, regular, scar, scholar, secular, similar, solar, sonar, spar, star, sugar, tar, tartar, triangular, tsar, tubular, ulnar, vehicular, vernacular, vicar, vinegar, vulgar

'ER' (OCCUPATIONS)

adviser, avenger, baker, banker, bartender, barterer, bookkeeper, bookseller, bowler, bricklayer, builder, butcher, buyer, carpenter, caterer, character, chopper, cooper, courier, dancer, daughter, debater, defaulter, designer, discoverer, docker, dressmaker, drifter, driver, executioner, exporter, farmer, fielder, fighter, flyer, furnisher, gaoler, gardener, grocer, hairdresser, hurdler, idolater, installer, ironmonger, joiner, launcher, lawyer, lender, maker, manager, master, mender, miser, murderer, organiser, painter, performer, photographer, plasterer, player, plumber, printer, producer, protester, publisher, qualifier, resister, rider, roofer, runner, seller, settler, sign-writer, singer, soldier, stationer, storyteller, swimmer, teacher, teller, tiler, walker, winner, worker, writer

'OR' (PERSON OR THING THAT)

actor, abettor, advisor, aerator, auditor, author, aviator, carburettor, censor, chancellor, compositor, compressor, conqueror, convector, councillor, counsellor, creator, creditor, curator, cursor, debtor, divisor, doctor, donor, duplicator, editor, emperor, erector, factor, governor, impostor, incisor, incubator, investor, jailor, juror, major, matador, mayor, mentor, orator, professor, prospector, rector, rotor, sailor, sector, senator, sensor, solicitor, spectator, sponsor, suitor, supervisor, suppressor, surveyor, tailor, tenor, tractor, tremor, tutor, vector, vendor, victor, visitor, visor, warrior

'OUR'

ardour, armour, behaviour, candour, clamour, colour, contour, demeanour, detour, endeavour, favour, flavour, harbour, honour, hour, humour, labour, neighbour, our, parlour, pompadour, rancour, rigour, savour, splendour, succour, troubadour, tumour, valour, vapour, vigour

'RE' (SOUNDING LIKE 'ER' OR 'UH')

acre, calibre, centimetre, centre, euchre, fibre, genre, goitre, litre, louvre, lucre, lustre, manoeuvre, massacre, meagre, mediocre, metre, millimetre, mitre, nitre, ochre, ogre, reconnoitre, sabre, saltpetre, sceptre, sepulchre, sombre, spectre, subgenre, theatre, titre, wiseacre

'ARY'

actuary, adversary, alimentary, ancillary, anniversary, antiquary, apiary, apothecary, arbitrary, auxiliary, aviary, axillary, beggary, beneficiary, bicentenary, binary, boundary, burglary, bursary, calvary, canary, capillary, cassowary, cautionary, centenary, commentary, complementary, complimentary, constabulary, contemporary, contrary, corollary, culinary, customary, delusionary, depositary, diary, dictionary, dietary, dignitary, disciplinary, dispensary, dromedary, elementary, emissary, estuary, evolutionary, exemplary, extemporary, extraordinary, February, fragmentary, friary, fritillary, glary, glossary, granary, hereditary, honorary, imaginary, incendiary, infirmary, insanitary, involuntary, itinerary, January, judiciary, lapidary, legendary, library, literary, mammary, mandatary, mercenary, military, millenary, missionary, monetary, mortuary, necessary, obituary, ordinary, ovary, parliamentary, pituitary, plenary, preliminary, primary, proprietary, reactionary, revolutionary, rosary, rotary, rudimentary, salary, salutary, sanctuary, sanitary, scary, secretary, sedentary, sedimentary, seminary, solitary, stationary, sugary, summary, supplementary, temporary, tertiary, topiary, tributary, unitary, urinary, vagary, vary, veterinary, visionary, vocabulary, voluntary, wary

'ERY'

adultery, archery, artillery, bakery, battery, blustery, bravery, brewery, bribery, buttery, cannery, cattery, celery, cemetery, chancellery, chancery, confectionery, cookery, crockery, cutlery, delivery, discovery, distillery, dithery, doddery, drapery, drudgery, dysentery, eatery, embroidery, emery, every, finery, fishery, flattery, flowery, gallery, gingery, glittery, greenery, grocery, gunnery, haberdashery, hosiery, imagery, jewellery, joinery, livery, lottery, machinery, microsurgery, mockery, monastery, mystery, nunnery, nursery, perfumery, periphery, piggery, pottery, powdery, query, recovery, refinery, robbery, rockery, saddlery, savagery, scenery, scullery, showery, shrubbery, skulduggery, slippery, spidery, stationery, surgery, swannery, tannery, tottery, treachery, upholstery, very, vinery, watery, winery, wintery

'ORY'

accessory, advisory, allegory, ambulatory, auditory, category, celebratory, chicory, compensatory, compulsory, congratulatory, conservatory, contradictory, contributory, cursory, defamatory, depository, derisory, desultory, directory, dormitory, dory, excretory, explanatory, factory, glory, gory, history, inflammatory, introductory, inventory, ivory, laboratory, lavatory, mandatory, memory, migratory, obligatory, observatory, oratory, pillory, precursory, predatory, preparatory, priory, promissory, purgatory, rectory, refectory, refractory, regulatory, respiratory, salutatory, satisfactory, sensory, signatory, statutory, story, supervisory, theory, tory, victory

'DOM'

bachelordom, boredom, chiefdom, Christendom, czardom, dukedom, earldom, freedom, hippiedom, kingdom, martyrdom, officialdom, princedom, random, saintdom, seldom, stardom, subkingdom, superstardom, wisdom

'FUL'

armful, awful, bagful, baleful, bashful, basketful, beautiful, bellyful, blissful, boastful, bountiful, boxful, brimful, bucketful, careful, cheerful, colourful, cupful, deceitful, delightful, disdainful, doleful, doubtful, dreadful, earful, eyeful, faithful, fanciful, fateful, fearful, fistful, forceful, forgetful, fruitful, gleeful, graceful, grateful, handful, helpful, hopeful, hurtful, jarful, joyful, lawful, manful, masterful, meaningful, merciful, mindful, mournful, mugful, painful, peaceful, pitiful, plentiful, pocketful, powerful, purposeful, regretful, remorseful, resentful, resourceful, restful, revengeful, shameful, sinful, skilful, sorrowful, spiteful, spoonful, stressful, successful, tactful, tankful, tasteful, thankful, thoughtful, truthful, ungrateful, watchful, wilful, woeful, wonderful, wrongful, youthful

'GRAPH'

allograph, autograph, autoradiograph, barograph, cardiograph, choreograph, chromatograph, chronograph, cinematograph, coronograph, cryptograph, digraph, electromyograph, encephalograph, epigraph, hectograph, heliograph, holograph, hygrograph, lithograph, micrograph, mimeograph, monograph, oscillograph, paragraph, photograph, photolithograph, pneumograph, polygraph, radiograph, radiotelegraph, rephotograph, seismograph, shadowgraph, spectrograph, stereograph, subparagraph, telegraph, thermograph, trigraph, xylograph

'HOOD'

adulthood, babyhood, bachelorhood, boyhood, brotherhood, childhood, falsehood, girlhood, knighthood, likelihood, livelihood, maidenhood, manhood, monkhood, neighbourhood, parenthood, priesthood, sisterhood, spinsterhood, statehood, unlikelihood, widowhood, widowerhood, womanhood

'IC'

acidic, acrobatic, aeronautic, alcoholic, algebraic, allergic, alphabetic, amoebic, angelic, Arabic, aristocratic, artistic, astronautic, athletic, atmospheric, atomic, autographic, automatic, basic, beatific, bibliographic, bionic, bombastic, characteristic, cherubic, colonic, comic, conic, critic, cubic, cyclonic, cynic, democratic, demonic, despotic, drastic, elliptic, enthusiastic, euphoric, evangelic, fantastic, feudalistic, frantic, futuristic, geometric, Germanic, gigantic, hemispheric, heroic, historic, holistic, horrific, humanistic, hygienic, Icelandic, iconic, idealistic, idiotic, idyllic, jingoistic, journalistic, Jurassic, kinetic, liguistic, logistic, magnetic, metallic, metaphoric, methodic, microscopic, naturalistic, oceanic, operatic, optimistic, patriotic, pedantic, phobic, photographic, poetic, protoplasmic, realistic, rhythmic, robotic, satanic, satiric, scenic, scholastic, specific, spheric, symmetric, terrific, tragic

'ING' (DROPPING THE 'E' BEFORE ADDING 'ING')

adoring, amusing, becoming, believing, charging, creating, debating, describing, educating, exciting, fining, forgiving, giving, grieving, hiking, hosing, improving, inflating, jiving, judging, kiting, liking, loving, managing, moving, navigating, noticing, operating, opposing, queuing (or queueing), rating, receiving, shaking, storing, tracing, tuning, uniting, using, valuing, verging, waving, whistling, zoning

'ING' (KEEPING THE 'E' BEFORE ADDING 'ING')

ageing (or aging), bingeing (or binging), canoeing, cueing (or cuing), dyeing, eyeing (or eying), glueing (or gluing), hoeing, shoeing, singeing, tingeing (or tinging), toeing, whingeing

also: agreeing, decreeing, disagreeing, fleeing, foreseeing, freeing, guaranteeing, kneeing, leveeing, overseeing, peeing, refereeing, seeing

'IVE'

abortive, abusive, adaptive, addictive, adoptive, alternative, argumentative, assertive, associative, attractive, aversive, collective, combustive, conductive, conflictive, cooperative, corrective, corruptive, decorative, defective, defensive, deflective, destructive, detective, digestive, dismissive, disruptive, distinctive, distractive, educative, elaborative, elective, eruptive, excessive, exhaustive, expensive, expletive, exploitive, explosive, figurative, imitative, impressive, intensive, inventive, massive, objective, obstructive, offensive, preventive, productive, progressive, protective, reclusive, reflective, regressive, repulsive, secretive, sedative, selective, speculative, suggestive, supportive, talkative

'L' AND 'LL'

annul	annulled	annulling	annulment
appal	appalled	appalling	
appeal	appealed	appealing	appealable
bevel	bevelled	bevelling	
cancel	cancelled	cancelling	
channel	channelled	channelling	
chisel	chiselled	chiselling	
compel	compelled	compelling	compulsion
counsel	counselled	counselling	
enrol	enrolled	enrolling	enrolment
expel	expelled	expelling	expulsion
fulfil	fulfilled	fulfilling	fulfilment
grovel	grovelled	grovelling	
impel	impelled	impelling	
instal	installed	installing	instalment
instil	instilled	instilling	instilment
label	labelled	labelling	
level	levelled	levelling	
marvel	marvelled	marvelling	marvellous
model	modelled	modelling	
panel	panelled	panelling	
parallel	paralleled	paralleling	
propel	propelled	propelling	
quarrel	quarrelled	quarrelling	quarrelsome
revel	revelled	revelling	revelry
shovel	shovelled	shovelling	shovelful
signal	signalled	signalling	signalman
travel	travelled	travelling	

'LESS'

ageless, aimless, airless, backless, baseless, beardless, boneless, bottomless, boundless, brainless, breathless, careless, ceaseless, characterless, cheerless, chinless, classless, cloudless, clueless, collarless, comfortless, cordless, countless, crewless, cuffless, defenceless, doubtless, effortless, endless, expressionless, faceless, faithless, fatherless, faultless, fearless, featureless, flawless, foamless, hairless, harmless, hatless, headless, heartless, heedless, heirless, helpless, homeless, hopeless, irregardless, jobless, joyless, lawless, lifeless, listless, loveless, luckless, meaningless, mindless, motherless, motionless, motiveless, nameless, needless, odourless, painless, pitiless, pointless, powerless, priceless, reckless, regardless, relentless, remorseless, restless, rimless, ruthless, seamless, senseless, shameless, shapeless, sleepless, smokeless, soulless, spineless, spotless, starless, strapless, talentless, tasteless, thankless, thoughtless, timeless, tireless, toothless, topless, treeless, tuneless, useless, weaponless, witless, worthless

'LY'

most words just add 'ly':
accidentally, actually, bashfully, beautifully, beneficially, carefully, colourfully, completely, coolly, cruelly, cynically, especially, eternally, eventually, extremely, faithfully, familiarly, finally, fitfully, fortunately, friendly, frightfully, fruitfully, generally, gradually, gratefully, helpfully, hopefully, humorously, immediately, incidentally, independently, interestingly, jokingly, joyfully, latterly, lethally, likely, lonely, lovely, loyally, meaningfully, mournfully, occasionally, paternally, peacefully, personally, pitifully, playfully, principally, quickly, quietly, radically, really, rigorously, separately, similarly, sincerely, sinfully, socially, staunchly, stupidly, successfully, tactfully, tearfully, thoughtfully, totally, usefully, usually, vigorously, vividly, wishfully, wonderfully

but:
words ending in 'y' change the 'y' to 'i'; for example:
angrily, busily, cosily, crazily, easily, funnily, greedily, happily, hazily, hungrily, lazily, merrily, momentarily, necessarily, ordinarily, readily, shabbily, steadily

and:
words ending in 'ic' add 'ally':
analytically, automatically, basically, characteristically, comically, critically, cynically, democratically, drastically, eccentrically, enthusiastically, fantastically, frantically, heroically, historically, horrifically, hygienically, hysterically, pathetically, rhythmically, scenically, scholastically, scientifically, specifically, statistically, stoically, symmetrically, terrifically, tragically

'MENT'

abasement, abatement, abolishment, accoutrement, achievement, acknowledgment, adjournment, adjustment, adornment, advancement, advertisement, agreement, ailment, alignment, allotment, amazement, amendment, amusement, announcement, annulment, anointment, apartment, appointment, argument, armament, arrangement, assessment, astonishment, atonement, attachment, attainment, augment, banishment, basement, bemusement, bereavement, bewilderment, bombardment, casement, catchment, cement, clement, commencement, comment, commitment, complement, compliment, concealment, condiment, contentment, curtailment, deferment, department, deployment, deportment, derailment, detachment, detriment, development, disappointment, document, easement, element, elopement, embankment, embarrassment, embellishment, embodiment, employment, enactment, encasement, encouragement, endearment, endowment, enforcement, enhancement, enjoyment, enlargement, enrichment, entertainment, entitlement, entrapment, environment, equipment, escarpment, excitement, excrement, experiment,

ferment, figment, filament, fitment, fragment, fulfilment, garment, government, harassment, impeachment, implement, imprisonment, incitement, inclement, increment, indorsement, infringement, instalment, instrument, investment, involvement, judgment (judgement), ligament, measurement, merriment, monument, movement, oddment, ointment, ornament, parliament, payment, pediment, pigment, placement, predicament, punishment, refinement, regiment, repayment, requirement, rudiment, sacrament, sediment, segment, sentiment, settlement, shipment, statement, temperament, tenement, testament, torment, tournament, treatment, vehement, vestment, wonderment, worriment

'NESS'

abruptness, acuteness, aptness, avidness, awareness, awfulness, awkwardness, badness, baldness, bitterness, brightness, calmness, cheapness, cheekiness, coldness, cosiness, coyness, craziness, darkness, deafness, dimness, dizziness, drabness, dryness, eagerness, emptiness, firmness, fitness, flatness, fogginess, fondness, freshness, fullness, fuzziness, gladness, greatness, greediness, happiness, hardness, harmlessness, harshness, haziness, helpfulness, holiness, grimness, idleness, joyfulness, keenness, kindness, knowingness, lameness, lateness, laxness, laziness, lightness, loneliness, loudness, loveliness, madness, meanness, meekness, mildness, nakedness, newness, numbness, openness, plainness, pureness, quickness, quietness, remoteness, richness, ruggedness, ruthlessness, sadness, sameness, scarceness, seriousness, shyness, slowness, softness, steepness, stillness, tameness, tidiness, ugliness, vastness, waviness, weakness, wetness

'OUS'

ambidextrous, amorous, analogous, androgynous, anomalous, anonymous, autonomous, bigamous, blasphemous, bulbous, callous, cantankerous, conterminous, couscous, covetous, credulous, dangerous, decorous, dextrous, diaphanous, enormous, fabulous, famous, ferrous, fibrous, fortuitous, fungous, garrulous, generous, gibbous, grievous, heinous, horrendous, humorous, indigenous, infamous, iniquitous, intravenous, jealous, joyous, lecherous, luminous, lustrous, marvellous, meticulous, mountainous, mucous, murderous, mutinous, nebulous, nervous, nitrous, numerous, obstreperous, odorous, onerous, oviparous, parlous, perilous, platitudinous, pompous, populous, porous, preposterous, querulous, rapturous, ravenous, resinous, ridiculous, rigorous, scurrilous, sedulous, solicitous, sonorous, stupendous, timorous, treacherous, tremulous, tumorous, ulcerous, venous, venturous, vigorous, viviparous, vociferous, wondrous

'EOUS'

aqueous, beauteous, bounteous, courageous, courteous, cretaceous, crustaceous, curvaceous, cutaneous, disadvantageous, erroneous, extraneous, gaseous, herbaceous, hideous, igneous, instantaneous, ligneous, miscellaneous, nacreous, nauseous, ochreous, outrageous, piteous, plenteous, predaceous, righteous, sebaceous, simultaneous, spontaneous, sulphureous, vitreous

'IOUS'

acrimonious, ambitious, amphibious, anxious, atrocious, audacious, auspicious, bilious, bumptious, capacious, cautious, censorious, ceremonious, commodious, conscious, contagious, contentious, copious, curious, curvacious, delicious, delirious, devious, dubious, envious, factious, factitious, fastidious, ferocious, flirtatious, furious, glorious, gracious, gregarious, harmonious, hilarious, illustrious, impecunious, impervious, impious, industrious, infectious, ingenious, injurious, invidious, judicious, laborious, lascivious, luxurious, malicious, melodious, mysterious, nefarious, notorious, noxious, nutritious, oblivious, obnoxious, obsequious, obvious, odious, officious, omnifarious, opprobrious, penurious, pervious, pious, precious, prestigious, previous, prodigious, rapacious, rebellious, religious, rumbustious, salubrious, sanctimonious, scrumptious, seditious, serious, silicious, spacious, spurious, studious, supercilious, suspicious, tedious, tenacious, tortious, vicarious, victorious, vivacious, voracious

'UOUS'

ambiguous, arduous, assiduous, congruous, conspicuous, contemptuous, contiguous, continuous, deciduous, fatuous, impetuous, incestuous, incongruous, inconspicuous, ingenuous, innocuous, mellifluous, nocuous, perspicuous, presumptuous, promiscuous, sensuous, strenuous, sumptuous, superfluous, tempestuous, tenuous, tortuous, tumultuous, unambiguous, unctuous, vacuous, virtuous, voluptuous

'PHONE'

earphone, gramophone, headphone, homophone, megaphone, microphone, saxophone, speakerphone, telephone, videophone, xylophone

'SCOPE'

cryoscope, electroscope, endoscope, epidiascope, episcope, gastroscope, gyroscope, horoscope, kaleidoscope, microscope, oscilloscope, periscope, stereoscope, telescope, thermoscope

'SHIP'

airmanship, airship, associateship, authorship, battleship, cadetship, censorship, chairmanship, championship, chiefship, citizenship, clerkship, collectorship, comradeship, containership, courtship, craftsmanship, dealership, deanship, dictatorship, directorship, eldership, fellowship, flagship, friendship, governorship, gunship, headship, heirship, internship, kingship, kinship, ladyship, landownership, listenership, lordship, marksmanship, membership, mentorship, musicianship, ownership, partnership, premiership, professorship, readership, receivership, relationship, rulership, scholarship, seamanship, spaceship, sponsorship, sportsmanship, starship, steamship, studentship, township, tranship, troopship, tutorship, twinship, vicarship, viewership, wardenship, wardship, warship, workmanship, worship

'SPHERE'

atmosphere, bathysphere, biosphere, chromosphere, exosphere, hemisphere, hydrosphere, ionosphere, lithosphere, mesosphere, photosphere, stratosphere, troposphere

'SURE'

assure, censure, closure, composure, disclosure, displeasure, enclosure, ensure, erasure, exposure, fissure, foreclosure, insure, leisure, measure, pressure, treasure, unsure

'TURE'

acupuncture, adventure, agriculture, aperture, architecture, capture, caricature, conjecture, couture, creature, culture, curvature, denture, departure, enrapture, expenditure, feature, fixture, forfeiture, fracture, furniture, future, gesture, horticulture, immature, indenture, infrastructure, juncture, lecture, ligature, literature, manufacture, mature, miniature, mixture, moisture, musculature, nature, nurture, overture, pasture, picture, posture, premature, puncture, rapture, rupture, scripture, sculpture, signature, stature, stricture, structure, temperature, texture, tincture, torture, venture, vesture, vulture

'SION' (ASION)

abrasion, corrasion, dissuasion, evasion, invasion, occasion, persuasion, pervasion

'SION' (ISION)

circumcision, collision, concision, decision, derision, division, elision, envision, excision, incision, indecision, precision, prevision, provision, revision, subdivision, supervision, television, vision

'SION' (OSION)

corrosion, eclosion, erosion, implosion, plosion

'SION' (USION)

affusion, allusion, collusion, conclusion, confusion, contusion, delusion, diffusion, disillusion, effusion, elusion, exclusion, extrusion, fusion, illusion, inclusion, infusion, intrusion, obtrusion, occlusion, perfusion, preclusion, prelusion, profusion, protrusion, reclusion, seclusion, suffusion, transfusion

'SION' (ANSION)

expansion, mansion, overexpansion, scansion

'SION' (ENSION)

apprehension, ascension, comprehension, condescension, dimension, dissension, distension, extension, intension, pension, prehension, recension, suspension, tension

'SION' (ERSION)

aspersion, aversion, conversion, dispersion, diversion, emersion, eversion, extroversion, immersion, interspersion, introversion, inversion, perversion, retroversion, reversion, submersion, subversion, version

'SION' (ASSION)

compassion, dispassion, impassion, passion

'SION' (ESSION)

accession, aggression, cession, compression, concession, confession, decompression, depression, digression, dispossession, expression, immunosuppression, impression, intercession, obsession, oppression, possession, precession, procession, profession, progression, recession, regression, repression, retrogression, secession, session, succession, suppression, transgression

'SION' (ISSION)

admission, commission, decommission, emission, fission, intermission, mission, omission, permission, readmission, remission, scission, submission, transmission

'SION' (USSION)

concussion, discussion, percussion, repercussion

'TION' (ATION)

abbreviation, abdication, abomination, accommodation, accusation, activation, adaptation, admiration, adoration, adulation, aeration, affixation, agitation, alienation, allocation, alteration, amputation, animation, annotation, aspiration, association, aviation, calculation, capitation, carnation, celebration, cessation, citation, civilization, classification, collation, combination, concentration, congregation, consideration, cooperation, coronation, creation, damnation, decimation, decoration, dedication, deflation, delegation, denegation, derivation, desolation, deviation, dictation, domination, donation, duration, education, elation, elevation, emigration, equation, estimation, evacuation, examination, explanation, fascination, federation, filtration, fixation, formation, foundation, generation, germination, gestation, glaciation, graduation, gyration, habitation, hesitation, imagination, imitation, information, innovation, investigation, invitation, irrigation, irritation, jubilation, lactation, liberation, limitation, lineation, medication, migration, moderation, motivation, mutation, narration, nation, navigation, nomination, numeration, obligation, occupation, operation, oration, ovation, plantation, population, predation, probation, publication, punctuation, quotation, radiation, ration, recreation, relation, relaxation, rotation, sanitation, sensation, separation, simulation, station, taxation, temptation, tessellation, toleration, undulation, vacation, validation, variation, vegetation, vibration, vocation, zonation

'TION' (ETION)

accretion, completion, concretion, deletion, depletion, discretion, excretion, indiscretion, repletion, secretion, suppletion

'TION' (OTION)

commotion, demotion, devotion, emotion, locomotion, lotion, motion, notion, potion, promotion

'TION' (ITION)

abolition, acquisition, addition, admonition, ambition, ammunition, apparition, apposition, attrition, audition, coalition, cognition, competition, composition, condition, contrition, decomposition, definition, demolition, dentition, deposition, disposition, edition, erudition, exhibition, expedition, exposition, extradition, fruition, ignition, imposition, indisposition, inhibition, inquisition, intuition,

juxtaposition, lenition, malnutrition, munition, nutrition, opposition, partition, petition, position, precognition, precondition, predisposition, preposition, presupposition, prohibition, proposition, recognition, rendition, repetition, requisition, sedition, superstition, supposition, tradition, transition, tuition, volition

'TION' (CTION)

abduction, action, addiction, affection, affliction, attraction, auction, benediction, bisection, collection, compunction, concoction, confection, conjunction, connection, contraction, convection, conviction, correction, deduction, defection, dejection, depiction, destruction, detection, diction, direction, dissection, distinction, ejection, election, eviction, faction, fiction, fraction, friction, function, induction, infection, injection, injunction, inspection, instruction, junction, objection, obstruction, olfaction, perfection, prediction, projection, protection, reaction, reduction, reflection, refraction, rejection, retraction, ruction, sanction, section, seduction, selection, subtraction, suction, traction, transaction, unction

'TION' (NTION)

abstention, attention, circumvention, contention, convention, detention, dissention, distention, inattention, indention, intention, intervention, invention, mention, prevention, retention

'TION' (PTION)

absorption, adaption, adoption, assumption, caption, conception, conscription, consumption, contraception, corruption, description, disruption, eruption, exception, exemption, gumption, inception, inscription, interception, interruption, perception, prescription, presumption, reception, redemption, resumption, subscription, transcription

'TIAN'

Alsatian, Christian, Croatian, Dalmatian, dietitian, Egyptian, fustian, gentian, Martian, tertian, titian, Venetian

'CIAN'

academician, acoustician, arithmetician, beautician, clinician, cosmetician, crucian, diagnostician, dietician, electrician, Grecian, logistician, magician, mechanician, mortician, musician, obstetrician, optician, paediatrician, patrician, phonetician, physician, politician, statistician, tactician, technician, theoretician

'XION'

axion, complexion, connexion, crucifixion, deflexion, flexion, fluxion, inflexion, reflexion, transfixion

'Y'

airy, baggy, beady, bitty, bony, bossy, bouncy, brainy, bristly, bubbly, bumpy, chatty, cheesly, chilly, cloudy, crafty, creepy, crispy, crumbly, crusty, cuddly, curly, dewy, dirty, dopy, dotty, drizzly, dusty, earthy, fatty, fiddly, filthy, fleecy, foggy, frilly, frosty, furry, fussy, giggly, glossy, grassy, greasy, greedy, grubby, hairy, healthy, hilly, icy, inky, jerky, juicy, knotty, lazy, leaky, lucky, marshy, messy, mighty, moody, muddy, noisy, nutty, oily, peppery, pricy, puffy, rainy, rosy, rusty, sandy, skinny, slimy, smelly, spooky, spotty, squeaky, stuffy, tasty, tricky, windy, witty, wrinkly

EXAMPLES OF WORDS THAT DOUBLE THEIR LAST LETTER BEFORE A SUFFIX BEGINNING WITH A VOWEL

a) Words of one syllable

bat	batted	batting
bed	bedded	bedding
beg	begged	begging
bet	betted	betting
clap	clapped	clapping
clip	clipped	clipping
cram	crammed	cramming
drag	dragged	dragging
drop	dropped	dropping
fit	fitted	fitting
fret	fretted	fretting
grip	gripped	gripping
hop	hopped	hopping
knit	knitted	knitting
knot	knotted	knotting
plan	planned	planning
plod	plodded	plodding
quit	quitted	quitting
quiz	quizzed	quizzing
rev	revved	revving
rub	rubbed	rubbing
scan	scanned	scanning
scrub	scrubbed	scrubbing
ship	shipped	shipping
sip	sipped	sipping
skip	skipped	skipping
slap	slapped	slapping
slip	slipped	slipping
squat	squatted	squatting
step	stepped	stepping
stop	stopped	stopping
tap	tapped	tapping
trap	trapped	trapping
trek	trekked	trekking
whip	whipped	whipping
yap	yapped	yapping

b) Words of more than one syllable where the stress is on the last syllable

acquit	acquitted	acquitting
admit	admitted	admitting
allot	allotted	allotting
begin	(began)	beginning
commit	committed	committing
confer	conferred	conferring
equip	equipped	equipping
forget	(forgot)	forgetting
occur	occurred	occurring
omit	omitted	omitting
permit	permitted	permitting
prefer	preferred	preferring
refer	referred	referring
transmit	transmitted	transmitting

c) Words that end in 'l' – no matter where the stress is

annul	annulled	annulling
appal	appalled	appalling
bevel	bevelled	bevelling
cancel	cancelled	cancelling
channel	channelled	channelling
compel	compelled	compelling
enrol	enrolled	enrolling
expel	expelled	expelling
fulfil	fulfilled	fulfilling
grovel	grovelled	grovelling
impel	impelled	impelling
instil	instilled	instilling
kennel	kennelled	kennelling
label	labelled	labelling
level	levelled	levelling
marvel	marvelled	marvelling
model	modelled	modelling
panel	panelled	panelling
propel	propelled	propelling
quarrel	quarrelled	quarrelling
revel	revelled	revelling
shovel	shovelled	shovelling
signal	signalled	signalling
travel	travelled	travelling
tunnel	tunnelled	tunnelling

EXAMPLES OF WORDS THAT END IN A SHORT VOWEL BUT DO NOT DOUBLE THE LAST LETTER BEFORE A SUFFIX BEGINNING WITH A VOWEL

a) Words that have two consonants after the short vowel

back	backed	backing
bang	banged	banging
bank	banked	banking
bump	bumped	bumping
camp	camped	camping
check	checked	checking
crack	cracked	cracking
dash	dashed	dashing
dent	dented	denting
drink	(drank)	drinking
dust	dusted	dusting
film	filmed	filming
flash	flashed	flashing
hang	(hung)	hanging
hint	hinted	hinting
jump	jumped	jumping
kick	kicked	kicking
knock	knocked	knocking
lack	lacked	lacking
lift	lifted	lifting
list	listed	listing
melt	melted	melting
nest	nested	nesting
pack	packed	packing
pelt	pelted	pelting
pick	picked	picking
risk	risked	risking
rock	rocked	rocking
rust	rusted	rusting
shift	shifted	shifting
smack	smacked	smacking
smash	smashed	smashing
test	tested	testing
trick	tricked	tricking
wink	winked	winking

b) Words of more than one syllable where the stress is on the first or earlier syllable

ballot	balloted	balloting
banquet	banqueted	banqueting
benefit	benefited	benefiting
billet	billeted	billeting
blanket	blanketed	blanketing
blossom	blossomed	blossoming
bracket	bracketed	bracketing
budget	budgeted	budgeting
carpet	carpeted	carpeting
chirrup	chirruped	chirruping
discomfort	discomforted	discomforting
ferret	ferreted	ferreting
fidget	fidgeted	fidgeting
fillet	filleted	filleting
focus	focused	focusing

gallop	galloped	galloping
gossip	gossiped	gossiping
happen	happened	happening
harvest	harvested	harvesting
hiccup	hiccuped	hiccuping
market	marketed	marketing
pilot	piloted	piloting
pivot	pivoted	pivoting
profit	profited	profiting
rivet	riveted	riveting
scallop	scalloped	scalloping
target	targeted	targeting

c) Words that end in 'x'

affix	affixed	affixing
annex	annexed	annexing
box	boxed	boxing
fax	faxed	faxing
fix	fixed	fixing
flex	flexed	flexing
index	indexed	indexing
mix	mixed	mixing
relax	relaxed	relaxing
remix	remixed	remixing
tax	taxed	taxing
telex	telexed	telexing
wax	waxed	waxing

EXAMPLES OF WORDS THAT END IN A CONSONANT BEFORE A 'Y'

beauty	beautiful, beautify
bury	buried, burying, buries
busy	busied, busying, busiest, busily, business
carry	carried, carrying, carrier, carries
comply	complied, complying, complies, compliant
copy	copied, copying, copies
deny	denied, denying, denies
dry	dried, drying, drier, driest
easy	easier, easiest, easily
fly	flew, flying, flies
funny	funnier, funniest, funnily
happy	happier, happiest, happily, happiness
hungry	hungrier, hungriest, hungrily
hurry	hurried, hurrying
imply	implied, implying, implication
justify	justified, justifying, justification
lazy	lazier, laziest, lazily
marry	married, marrying, marriage
merry	merrier, merriest, merriment
occupy	occupied, occupying, occupies
pity	pitied, pitying, pities, pitiful, pitiless
pretty	prettier, prettiest, prettily, prettiness
rely	relied, relying, relies, reliant
reply	replied, replying, replies
shady	shadier, shadiest
spy	spied, spying, spies
study	studied, studying, studies, studious
tasty	tastier, tastiest
try	tried, trying, tries
vary	varied, varying, variance
worry	worried, worrying, worries

Hyphens and suffixes

A hyphen is used to form compound words (a habit from our Anglo-Saxon ancestors). Once the word has been in use for some time, however, the hyphen is often dropped.

Some common examples of words where hyphens can be used are given below. However, it is often a case of what is fashionable (ie to use a hyphen or not), rather than which is 'right' or 'wrong'.

-ALL

carry-all, catch-all, cure-all, end-all, free-for-all, hold-all, know-all

-AWAY

give-away

-BACK

back-to-back, button-back, carry-back, fall-back, ladder-back, laid-back,

-BY

by-and-by, lay-by, stand-by

-DOWN

broken-down, close-down, let-down, low-down, put-down, run-down, sit-down, slow-down, take-down, thumbs-down, top-down, two-down, up-and-down, upside-down

-FREE

duty-free, fancy-free, hands-free, lead-free, nuclear-free, rent-free, scot-free

-IN

built-in, check-in, drive-in, hand-in, lead-in, phone-in, plug-in, pull-in, read-in, run-in, shut-in, sit-in, sitter-in, stand-in, take-in, teach-in, throw-in, trade-in

-LESS

A hyphen is used when 'less' is added to a word that already ends in 'll', such as:

shell-less, skill-less, smell-less, wall-less

-LIKE

A hyphen is used when 'like' is added to a word that already ends in 'll', such as:

shell-like, tail-like, wall-like

-OFF

brush-off, cut-off, far-off, hands-off, kick-off, lay-off, lift-off, pay-off, play-off, rip-off, show-off, stand-off, take-off, tip-off, trade-off, turn-off, well-off, write-off

-ON

carry-on, clip-on, come-on, follow-on, goings-on, hanger-on, head-on, knock-on, pull-on, put-on, roll-on, slip-on, try-on, turn-on, walk-on

-OUT

check-out, cut-out, fall-out, far-out, hand-out, hide-out, line-out, pull-out, read-out, rig-out, shake-out, share-out, shoot-out, shut-out, throw-out, try-out, walk-out, wash-out, way-out, white-out, wipe-out

-OVER

change-over, flash-over, going-over, once-over, push-over, switch-over, up-and-over, voice-over, walk-over

-UP

blow-up, brush-up, build-up, bust-up, buttoned-up, call-up, carve-up, check-up, clean-up, close-up, cock-up, dust-up, fill-up, fit-up, flare-up, follow-up, foul-up, frame-up, freeze-up, fry-up, get-up, hang-up, hold-up, hook-up, knock-up, line-up, link-up, lock-up, make-up, mark-up, mix-up, mock-up, paid-up, paste-up, pick-up, pile-up, pin-up, pop-up, press-up, punch-up, push-up, put-up, round-up, run-up, set-up, shake-up, slap-up, smash-up, snarl-up, speed-up, stand-up, summing-up, thumbs-up, tie-up, tip-up, toss-up, turn-up, two-up, warm-up, washing-up, wind-up, write-up

Spelling activities – suffixes

1   Provide the children with a list of root words, such as: play, happy, delight, fresh, harm, worth, pity and colour. Challenge them to use dictionaries to find as many suffixes as they can to attach to these words. Make class lists for the children to add to over the week.

   For example: play

   player, played, playing, playful, playable, playfully, playfulness, playlet, play-acting, playback, playsome, playboy, play-day, played-out, playground, playgroup, playhouse, playleader, playmate, play-off, playpen, playschool, playroom, playsuit,
plaything, playtime

2   Have fun with atlases and maps by asking the children to find place names that a particular suffix, such as 'ford' or 'ham'.

3   Make a circle with a spinning arrow. Divide the circle into sections with a different suffix in each. The children take it in turns to spin the arrow. They have to write down a word that has that suffix. Use dictionaries to check spellings. They can earn two points for a correct word and a further two points for the correct spelling of the word.

4   Play 'Suffix bingo'. Provide each child with a grid containing suffixes (be careful to use suffixes that do not sound alike). (The children could copy the suffixes into their own grids so that each grid will be different.) Call out words some of which contain one of the suffixes and some of which that don't. The children have to listen to the words and place a counter on the appropriate suffix. The first player to have five in a row is the winner.

ing	hood	ship	ly	able
shere	graph	ist	gram	poly
dom	ery	ant	age	itis
scope	ful	ness	meter	some
ology	ic	tion	sis	ment

5   Explore the suffix 'er', meaning 'one who', by making a class book of occupations. Begin by having a word hunt to find lots of occupations that end in 'er' (use the list on page 54 to help you). The book could be set out like a reference dictionary with the words in alphabetical order, together with a definition of each word, related words and illustrations.

Plurals

Plural rules

Some of the most useful rules to learn are those dealing with plurals because once you learn them you can apply them to unfamiliar words with confidence!

1 Most nouns just add 's'.
Most nouns are made plural (more than one) by simply adding 's'. For example:

ant	ants
book	books
clock	clocks
drum	drums
elephant	elephants

This is also a safe rule for words that end in 'e'. For example:

athlete	athletes
bike	bikes
circle	circles
disease	diseases
engine	engines

2 Words that end in 'ch', 'sh', 's', 'ss', 'x', 'z' or 'zz', add 'es'.
For example:

church	churches
dish	dishes
atlas	atlases
class	classes
fox	foxes
waltz	waltzes
buzz	buzzes

But note:

quiz	quizzes
ox	oxen

Exceptions

a Some words that end in 's' (usually of foreign origin or foreign influence) do not follow this rule. For example:

alumnus	alumni
analysis	analyses
antithesis	antitheses
axis	axes
basis	bases
crisis	crises
diagnosis	diagnoses
ellipsis	ellipses
genus	genera
hypothesis	hypotheses
means	means
metamorphosis	metamorphoses
oasis	oases
parenthesis	parentheses
series	series
stimulus	stimuli
thesis	theses

Other words in the group can have two or more accepted forms of the plural. For example:

apex	apexes or apices
appendix	appendixes or appendices
cactus	cactuses or cacti
corpus	corpora
crocus	crocuses
crux	cruxes or cruces
fish	fishes or fish
focus	focuses or foci
fungus	funguses or fungi
genius	geniuses or genii
gladiolus	gladioluses or gladioli
helix	helixes or helices
ibex	ibex, ibexes or ibices
index	indexes or indices
iris	irises or irides
matrix	matrixes or matrices
nucleus	nucleuses or nuclei
radius	radiuses or radii
syllabus	syllabuses or syllabi
terminus	terminuses or termini
vortex	vortexes or vortices

b 'ch' words that make a hard 'c' sound, such as epoch, loch, matriarch, monarch, patriarch and stomach, just add 's'.

3 Words that end in 'y'

a If there is a vowel before the 'y', just add 's'. For example:

bay	bays
buy	buys
convoy	convoys
valley	valleys

b If there is a consonant before the 'y', change the 'y' to 'i' and then add 'es'. For example:

baby	babies
fly	flies
tragedy	tragedies

Exceptions

Proper nouns ending in a consonant plus 'y' (for example, family names) do not change the 'y' to 'i' and add 'es' they just add 's'. For example: The Barrys are moving to London.

4 Words that end in 'f', or 'fe', normally change the 'f' or 'fe' to 'v' and then add 'es'.

For example:

calf	calves
knife	knives
thief	thieves
wife	wives

Exceptions

a   Some words just add 's'. For example:

aperitif	aperitifs
belief	beliefs
brief	briefs
cafe	cafes
chef	chefs
chief	chiefs
coif	coifs
dwarf	dwarfs (rare – dwarves)
gulf	gulfs
motif	motifs
oaf	oafs (rare – oaves)
proof	proofs
reef	reefs
roof	roofs
safe	safes
serf	serfs
serif	serifs
shaduf	shadufs
waif	waifs
woof	woofs

b   Words that end in 'ff' just add 's'. For example:

cuff	cuffs
muff	muffs
staff	staffs
tariff	tariffs

Some words have two acceptable spellings. For example:

handkerchief	handkerchiefs or handkerchieves
hoof	hoofs or hooves
scarf	scarfs or scarves
turf	turfs or turves
wharf	wharfs or wharves

5 Words that end in 'o'

a   If there is a vowel before the 'o', just add 's'. For example:

cameo	cameos
kangaroo	kangaroos
radio	radios
scenario	scenarios
zoo	zoos

b   If the word is a noun that has been abbreviated, just add 's'. For example:

auto	autos
disco	discos
kilo	kilos
memo	memos
micro	micros
photo	photos

c   If the word is a musical term usually just add 's'. For example:
alto, banjo, cello, concerto, crescendo, libretto, piano, piccolo, solo, soprano

d   If there is a consonant before the 'o', some words add 's' and others add 'es'. Apart from the two rules above (abbreviations and musical terms) there is no general rule to help you distinguish between the two groups. It is a matter of learning the plurals of these words.

Words that just add an 's':
albinos, armadillos, avocados, boleros, cantos, casinos, commandos, dynamos, egos, embryos, gauchos, giros, gringos, infernos, kimonos, machos, maraschinos, palolos, palominos, ponchos, pros, silos, sombreros, stilettos, tacos, tangos, torsos

Words that add 'es':
buffaloes, echoes, embargoes, heroes, magnificoes, Negroes, potatoes, tomatoes, vetoes

Words that can end in 's' or 'es':
archipelago, bravo, cargo, desperado, dodo, domino, fiasco, flamingo, fresco, gazebo, ghetto, grotto, hobo, indigo, innuendo, lasso, mango, manifesto, memento, mosquito, motto, mulatto, no, palmetto, peccadillo, placebo, proviso, tiro (tyro), tobacco, tornado, torpedo, volcano, zero

Note: buffalo can be both singular and plural.

The plural of embryo can be embryos or embryons. The plural of torso can be torsos or (rarely) torsi.

6 **Some words are the same in the singular and the plural.**
For example:
aircraft, cattle, cod, deer, fish (or fishes), grouse, moose, police, pike, salmon, series, sheep, species, swine, trout

7 **Some nouns generally occur in the plural form only.**
For example:
binoculars, breeches, forceps, glasses (spectacles), goods, jeans, oats, pants, pliers, police, pyjamas, scissors, shears, shorts, tongs, trousers, tweezers

8 **Some words look plural, but should be treated as singular.**
For example:
athletics, economics, gymnastics, logistics, mathematics, politics

9 **Compound words**
Words that are hyphenated usually form the plural by adding 's' to the most important word.
For example:

lady-in-waiting	ladies-in-waiting
looker-on	lookers-on
man-of-war	men-of-war
mother-in-law	mothers-in-law
passer-by	passers-by

But, if the word 'man' or 'woman' is the first part of a compound word consisting of two nouns, both parts of the word take the plural.
For example:

woman-worker	women-workers

Commonly, however, it is the last part of a compound word that takes the plural form.
For example:

by-election	by-elections
cross-reference	cross-references
knick-knack	knick-knacks
lay-by	lay-bys
major-general	major-generals
take-off	take-offs

10 **Words of a foreign origin can have a special plural form.**
For example:

addendum	addenda
alumna	alumnae
antenna	antennae
chateau	chateaux
corrigendum	corrigenda
criterion	criteria
datum	data
desideratum	desiderata
erratum	errata
maximum	maxima
minimum	minima
phenomenon	phenomena

(See also page 72.)

They can also have two accepted forms of the plural. For example:

alkali	alkalis or alkalies
bureau	bureaus or bureaux
concerto	concertos or concerti
crematorium	crematoriums or crematoria
curriculum	curriculums or curricula
dilettante	dilettantes or dilettanti
formula	formulas or formulae
gymnasium	gymnasiums or gymnasia
larva	larvae
mausoleum	mausoleums or mausolea
medium	mediums or media
memorandum	memorandums or memoranda
plateau	plateaus or plateaux
referendum	referendums or referenda
sanatorium	sanatoriums or sanatoria
spectrum	spectra
stratum	stratums or strata
tableau	tableaus or tableaux
virtuoso	virtuosos or virtuosi

(See also page 72.)

11 **Some words have an irregular plural form.**
For example:

child	children
foot	feet
goose	geese
louse	lice
man	men
mouse	mice
ox	oxen
penny	pence (meaning units of value)
tooth	teeth
woman	women

Useful words lists

'CH' NOUNS

approach, arch, batch, beach, belch, bench, bitch, blotch, branch, brooch, bunch, catch, church, clutch, coach, cockroach, couch, crunch, crutch, dispatch, ditch, finch, hatch, hitch, hunch, inch, itch, latch, leech, lunch, march, match, notch, ostrich, patch, paunch, peach, perch, pinch, porch, pouch, punch, ranch, sandwich, scratch, scotch, search, speech, splotch, stitch, stretch, switch, torch, trench, watch, wench, witch, wrench, wretch

'SH' NOUNS

ambush, ash, backlash, bash, blemish, blush, brush, bulrush, bush, clash, crash, crayfish, crush, dash, dogfish, eyelash, eyewash, finish, fish, flash, flourish, flush, gash, hairbrush, jellyfish, lash, leash, macintosh, parish, polish, push, radish, rash, rush, slash, splash, starfish, stash, swish, wash, wish

'S' NOUNS

atlas, bias, bus, census, gas, hiatus, lens

'SS' NOUNS

abscess, abyss, actress, address, albatross, ass, boss, brass, bypass, carcass, class, compass, countess, cross, cuss, cutlass, dress, duchess, excess, eyewitness, glass, goddess, grass, guess, harness, headdress, heiress, highness, hiss, hostess, kiss, lass, lioness, loss, mass, mistress, moss, pass, press, princess, recess, stress, success, tigress, toss, truss, witness

'X' NOUNS

annex, apex, appendix, box, climax, crucifix, equinox, fax, flax, flex, fox, gearbox, hoax, ibex, index, jukebox, lynx, matchbox, onyx, phlox, phoenix, postbox, sex, sphinx, suffix, tax, thorax, vortex, wax

'Z' AND 'ZZ' NOUNS

blitz, chintz, kibbutz, quartz, quiz, waltz
buzz, whizz

'AY' NOUNS

affray, airway, alleyway, array, ashtray, bay, byway, castaway, causeway, chardonnay, clay, cutaway, day, delay, display, doorway, dray, driveway, essay, foray, gangway, giveaway, hallway, highway, holiday, inlay, jay, motorway, nay, nosegay, passageway, pathway, play, quay, railway, ray, relay, replay, runway, screenplay, spray, stairway, stray, subway, takeaway, underlay, way, weekday, x-ray, yesterday

'EY' NOUNS

abbey, alley, attorney, barley, chimney, chutney, curtsey, donkey, galley, grey, hackney, honey, jersey, jockey, joey, journey, key, kidney, medley, monkey, osprey, pulley, spinney, storey, survey, trolley, turkey, turnkey, valley, volley

'OY' AND 'UY' NOUNS

alloy, boy, buoy, convoy, corduroy, cowboy, decoy, envoy, joy, killjoy, lowboy, pageboy, ploy, saveloy, schoolboy, tomboy, toy, viceroy
buy, guy

CONSONANT + 'Y' NOUNS

ability, academy, activity, agency, allergy, ally, amenity, anomaly, anthology, anxiety, army, assembly, authority, baby, battery, berry, body, bully, butterfly, casualty, cavity, celebrity, charity, cherry, city, comedy, community, conspiracy, copy, country, county, currency, curry, dairy, daisy, democracy, deputy, diary, difficulty, dolly, duty, dynasty, eighty, elegy, embassy, emergency, enemy, enquiry, facility, fairy, family, fantasy, ferry, festivity, flurry, fly, gallery, gantry, gully, gypsy, hobby, identity, impurity, inquiry, jalopy, jelly, jetty, jury, lady, levy, locality, lorry, lullaby, melody, ministry, monastery, mystery, nanny, nappy, novelty, opportunity, pansy, party, pastry, penalty, penny, pony, quantity, query, rally, redundancy, remedy, reply, responsibility, ruby, similarity, spy, story, strategy, study, supply, technology, teddy, tendency, tragedy, utility, vacancy, worry

'F' NOUNS

aperitif, belief, bookshelf, brief, calf, chef, chief, dwarf, elf, gulf, half, hoof, leaf, loaf, misbelief, motif, proof, reef, relief, roof, scarf, self, serf, serif, shaduf, sheaf, shelf, sunroof, thief, turf, waif, werewolf, wharf, wolf

'FE' NOUNS

cafe, giraffe, knife, life, midwife, penknife, safe, wife

'FF' NOUNS

bailiff, bluff, castoff, chuff, cliff, cuff, earmuff, flagstaff, gaff, handcuff, huff, kickoff, lay-off, muff, payoff, plaintiff, puff, scuff, sheriff, sniff, staff, takeoff, tariff, tiff, toff, whiff

Spelling activities – plurals

1. Play plural card games. Write the singular and plural forms of the words you want the children to learn on separate cards. Play the following games:

   a Individual timed game. How fast can they match the singular to the plural form? Use a stopwatch and record results. The children can aim to beat their previous times.

   b Individual memory game. Place the cards with singular words face down in rows (for example, four rows of four words) and the plural forms in a similar pattern next to them. The player turns over one card from each set with the aim of matching a singular with a plural form. Can they successfully remember where the words are?

   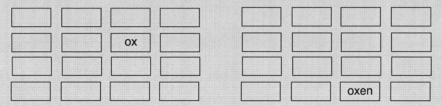

   c Paired game. One player has the singular words; the other has the plurals of these words. They can play snap, matching the singular to its plural form.

2. Make a class dictionary of plurals. Each child or pair could be responsible for a page. Each entry should contain the word in the singular and plural forms plus a definition. They could also illustrate the words and write them in a sentence.

3. Ask the children to make a picture book of plurals for younger children. The book could contain pictures of animals, for example, with a picture of one animal on a page and several of the same animal on the facing page. A good book to look at as an example is *Animal Families* by Colin Threadgall, 1996, Julia MacRae Books (Random House).

4. Play hangman where all the words have to be plurals. You could concentrate on specific rules each time to help reinforce them.

5. Ask the children to add to a word wall over time. Provide them with a starter collection of words for a specific plural spelling rule; for example: batch, church, patch, sandwich, wrench (adding 'es' to words that end in 'ch') and ask the children to find more words that belong to the group. The word wall could last for several weeks. Both the singular and plural forms should be written. How many 'ch' words can they find?

6. Have fun making up nonsense sentences to help the children remember the plurals of trickier words.

   For example:
   The **lice** on the **mice** quickly hid when they heard the **feet** of the **geese**.
   The **hippos** and **rhinos** took **photos** of the **armadillos**.

Chapter 9

Tricky spellings

Just why are some words tricky to spell? And why do we get easily confused over some words? There are five main reasons:

1 The English language contains many words that sound similar but have different spellings and meanings. These words are called 'homophones' (for example: one, won).
2 Some words look similar (for example: through and thorough).
3 Some words contain confusing sounds (for example: breath and breathe).
4 Some words are commonly misused because their meanings are not understood (for example: accept and except).
5 Some words originate from foreign languages and, therefore, do not follow the usual spelling rules (for example: déjà vu).

And sometimes there are words that we just seem to have a mental block with! These are the words that just never seem to look right when we write them down. These words (and some of YOUR tricky words may appear on our list on pages 79–80) need to be carefully committed to memory and often the use of mnemonics is the best way to remember them.

HOMOPHONES

Homophones are words that sound the same but have different spellings and meanings. The following are perhaps the most commonly confused homophones:

> two, to, too
> here, hear
> passed, past
> there, their, they're
> your, you're
> its, it's
> whose, who's

The best way to differentiate between the words is to commit their meanings to memory. You need to concentrate on one word at a time, learn its meaning and understand how the word is used. Teach yourself some useful mnemonics to help you remember their meanings, for example:

> You h**ear** with your **ear**s.
> H**ere**, th**ere** and everywh**ere**.
> > (All place words end in 'ere'.)
> At **last** he walked p**ast**!

Some common homophones

ad, add	draw, drawer
air, heir	drier, dryer
aisle, I'll, isle	dual, duel
allowed, aloud	earn, urn
altar, alter	ewe, yew, you
annex, annexe	eye, I
arc, ark	faint, feint
ate, eight	fair, fare
ball, bawl	feat, feet
bare, bear	fir, fur
be, bee	flea, flee
beach, beech	flew, flu, flue
bean, been	flour, flower
beat, beet	for, fore, four
bite, byte	fort, fought
blew, blue	forth, fourth
board, bored	foul, fowl
boarder, border	freeze, frieze
bough, bow	gait, gate
boy, buoy	gilt, guilt
brake, break	gorilla, guerilla
bread, bred	grate, great
brews, bruise	grisly, grizzly
bridal, bridle	groan, grown
buy, by, bye	guessed, guest
calendar, calender	hail, hale
canvas, canvass	hair, hare
carat, caret, carrot	hall, haul
ceiling, sealing	hart, heart
cellar, seller	hay, hey
cell, sell	heal, heel, he'll
cent, scent, sent	hear, here
cents, sense	heard, herd
cereal, serial	hi, high
cheap, cheep	higher, hire
check, cheque	him, hymn
chews, choose	hoar, whore
cite, sight, site	hoard, horde
coarse, course	hoarse, horse
coat, cote	hoes, hose
complementary, complimentary	hole, whole
	hour, our
council, counsel	idle, idol
creak, creek	in, inn
currant, current	it's, its
days, daze	jam, jamb
dear, deer	key, quay
dependant, dependent	knead, kneed, need
dew, due	knew, new
die, dye	knight, night
doe, dough	knot, not
done, dun	know, no
draft, draught	knows, nose

lead, led
leak, leek
lessen, lesson
liar, lyre
licence, license
lie, lye
loan, lone
made, maid
mail, male
main, mane
manner, manor
meat, meet
medal, meddle
meter, metre
might, mite
mind, mined
missed, mist
moor, more
moose, mousse
naval, navel
none, nun
oar, or, ore
oh, owe
one, won
paced, paste
pail, pale
pain, pane
pair, pare, pear
passed, past
patience, patients
pause, paws
peace, piece
peak, peek
peal, peel
pedal, peddle
peer, pier
place, plaice
plain, plane
pole, poll
poor, pore, pour
praise, prays, preys
pray, prey
presence, presents
principal, principle
prise, prize
program, programme
propellant, propellent
quarts, quartz
rain, reign, rein
raise, rays, raze
rap, wrap
read, red
real, reel
right, rite, wright,
  write
ring, wring
road, rode, rowed
role, roll
root, route
rose, rows
rough, ruff

rung, wrung
sail, sale
saw, soar, sore
scene, seen
sea, see
seam, seem
seas, sees, seize
sew, so, sow
shear, sheer
shoe, shoo
shore, sure
side, sighed
sole, soul
some, sum
son, sun
stair, stare
stairs, stares
stake, steak
stationary, stationery
steal, steel
storey, story
straight, strait
suite, sweet
sundae, Sunday
tacks, tax
tail, tale
taught, taut
tea, tee
team, teem
teas, tease, tees
their, there, they're
theirs, there's
threw, through
throne, thrown
thyme, time
tide, tied
tire, tyre
to, too, two
toad, towed
told, tolled
troop, troupe
vain, vane, vein
wade, weighed
waist, waste
wait, weight
waive, wave
ware, wear, where
way, weigh
we, wee
weak, week
weather, wether,
  whether
weave, we've
we'd, weed
which, witch
whine, wine
who's, whose
wood, would
yore, your, you're
you'll, yule

SOME COMMONLY CONFUSED WORDS

Some words are confused because their meanings are unclear to the person who is using them. In order to prevent this from happening, it is vital to learn the meanings of the individual words and understand how they are used. Some commonly confused words include:

accept	to take what someone offers you
except	to exclude, not including
advice	(noun) an opinion or information given
advise	(verb) to inform, recommend
affect	(verb) to alter, cause a change
effect	(noun) the result of an action (verb) to bring about
aural	relating to the ear
oral	relating to the mouth
bought	from 'to buy'
brought	from 'to bring'
breath	(noun) the air drawn into the lungs
breathe	(verb) to take in air
choose	to take one thing instead of another
chose	past tense of choose
dairy	where milk is produced
diary	a daily account
desert	(noun) a barren place (verb) to abandon
dessert	(noun) a sweet
elicit	(verb) to draw forth
illicit	(adjective) unlawful
emigrant	one who leaves a country to live elsewhere
immigrant	one who comes to live in a country
eminent	important, distinguished
imminent	about to happen
enquiry	a request for information
inquiry	an official investigation
ensure	to make sure
insure	to take out insurance
formally	ceremoniously
formerly	previously
lightening	(verb) making lighter
lightning	(noun) a flash of light in a storm

loose	(adjective) slack, not secure
lose	(verb) to fail to keep
personal	(adjective) private
personnel	(noun) employees or staff
quiet	(adjective) not making a noise
quite	(adverb) entirely, actually

Sometimes there is confusion between words with 'all' in them. For example:

already (meaning previously) and
all ready (meaning everyone/everything is ready)

altogether (meaning completely) and
all together (meaning everything or everyone is in one group)

always (meaning every time) and
all ways (meaning all of the ways)

COMMONLY MISSPELLED OR TRICKY WORDS

accept	archaeology
accidentally	arctic
accommodation	arguing/argument
accumulate	article
achieve	atmosphere
acquaintance	attach
acquire	aubergine
across	auxiliary
address	awful
adequate	
advertisement	balance
affect	bargain
aggravate	basically
aggression	beautifully
agitator	beginning
agreeable	believe
alleluia	beneficial
among	benefited
apostrophe	building
appalling	burglar
appear	business

calendar	exhilarating
carcass	existence
careful	expedient
carefully	expense
cemetery	experience
centuries	extravagant
chameleon	extremely
character	
chimneys	family
coming	fastening
committed	favourite
committee	February
comparison	fillip
completely	finish
comptroller	forbade
conceited	foreign
concentrate	foreigner
conscientious	forest
conscious	forty
consensus	fourteen
conspiracy	friend
contiguous	fulfil
convenience	fulfilled
courageous	
courgette	gaol
coxswain	gauge
criticism	government
	gradually
deceit	grammar
decision	grateful
defence	guild
definite	guillotine
descend	
description	
desiccate	
desperately	
detached	
developed	
development	
dextrous	
diarrhoea	
different	
disappear	haemorrhage
disastrous	haemorrhoids
doesn't	happened
drastically	harass
drunkenness	hearken
duly	height
	hiccup
ecstasy	honourable
effect	humorous
eighth	hypocrisy
elegant	
embarrass	idiosyncrasy
encyclopaedia	immediately
environment	incidentally
exaggerate	independent
excellent	intellectual
except	interested
excitement	interrupt
exciting	inveigle
exercise	involved
exhibit	

jalopy
jeopardy
jewellery

knowledge
knowledgeable
koala

laboratory
lacquer
laid
largess (or largesse)
lasso
leisure
liaison
library
lightning
likelihood
liquefy
liquorice
loneliness
loose
lose

maintenance
manageable
manoeuvre
margarine
marriage
marvellous
meanness
medicine
medieval
merely
minute
miracle
miscellaneous
mischievous
murmuring
myrrh

necessary
neighbours
ninth
no one
noticeable
novitiate (or noviciate)
occasion

occasionally
occurred
occurrence
offered
omelette (or omelet)
opportunity
opposition

paediatric
paid
palaeography
panicked
paraffin
parallel
parliament
particularly
passed
past
peony
permanent
permitted
perseverance
persistence
physically
picnicking
politician
pomegranate
possession
potatoes
practice
practise
preferred
prejudice
preparation
primitive
principal
principle
privilege
probably
procedure
proceed
professor
proletariat
promissory
publicly
pursue
putrefy
pyjamas

quarrelling
quarter
questionnaire
queue

rarefaction
rarefy
really
receive
recognise
recommend
recompense
referring
relevant
religious
restaurant
rhyme
rhythm
ridiculous

scallop
scene
schedule
schizophrenia
secretary
seize
sentence
separate
similarly
sincerely
singeing (burning lightly)
skiing
skilful
skilfully
solicitor
subtly
successfully
supersede
surprise
sycamore

taxiing
technique
temperature
temporary
terrifically
they're
thorough
timpani
tingeing (or tinging)

tomatoes
tomorrow
tragedy
tranquillity
traveller
tries
truly
twelfth
tying
tyranny

undoubtedly
unforgettable
unnecessary
until

valleys
vegetable
vehicle
veranda
vermilion
vicious
view
visitor
visor

Wednesday
weird
welfare
whether
wholly
who's
wistaria
withhold
woollen
worshipped
wrapping
writ

yacht
yield
you're

Spelling activities – learning tricky words

1. Write the tricky words on separate cards. Play various games with them each week to reinforce the correct spellings. These games can include:

   a Putting the words in dictionary order. How fast can this be done? A partner could use a stopwatch to time it.

   b Making two sets of the same words and playing snap with a partner or memory games such as game 1b on page 76.

   c Picking out three (or more) cards from the pack and writing a sentence using all the words!

   d Playing racing games with a partner, such as picking a card each from their own pack and then racing to see who can find it first in their dictionary. Score points for the quickest. Their partner must check that the word they found matches the one on the card. This game helps develop visual memory.

2. Make up sentences to help you remember words commonly confused. For example:

   Do not lose that l**oo**se t**oo**th.

   Personn**e**l are employ**ee**s but their person**a**l things still need to be priv**a**te.

3. Make a 'My tricky words' book for each child where particularly problematic words are listed alphabetically. This can be used as a reference when writing. Encourage the children to 'delete the demons' as quickly as possible by rewarding them for learning the words.

4. Reinforce commonly misspelled words by using them in handwriting activities on a regular basis.

5. Have fun learning a difficult word by overusing it. For example, ask the children to write a paragraph using the word 'eighth' as many times as possible.

   At the eighth hour on the eighth day of the eighth month, eight children sat down for the eighth time to eat eight cakes. The eight children were the eighth group to eat the eight cakes at the eighth hour on the eighth day of the eighth month so they earned eighty pounds, the eighth highest prize ever given.

6. Play 'What's missing?' Write a commonly misspelled word with the tricky part of the word missing. Can the children spot the error?

   For example: goverment (gover**n**ment)
   liason (lia**i**son)
   Febuary (Feb**r**uary)
   acommodation (ac**c**ommodation)

7. Play '1, 2 or 3?' Write the same word on three pieces of paper, but only one spelled correctly. Give a word each to three children. Number the children 1, 2 and 3. Ask them to show their words to the others at the same time. How quickly can the others spot the correctly spelled word? They need to shout out '1', '2' or '3'.

Spelling rule	Addressed		Comments
	Yes	No	
Looking at words	☐	☐	_____
Word shapes	☐	☐	_____
Mnemonics	☐	☐	_____
Syllables	☐	☐	_____
Compound words	☐	☐	_____
Words within words	☐	☐	_____
Alphabetical order	☐	☐	_____
Homonyms	☐	☐	_____
Guide words	☐	☐	_____
Proofreading	☐	☐	_____
'ie' and 'ei' words	☐	☐	_____
Silent letters	☐	☐	_____
Hard and soft 'c'	☐	☐	_____
Hard and soft 'g	☐	☐	_____
Apostrophe – contractions	☐	☐	_____
Apostrophe – possession	☐	☐	_____
Capital letters	☐	☐	_____
Short 'a' words	☐	☐	_____
Long 'a' words	☐	☐	_____
Short 'e' words	☐	☐	_____
Long 'e' words	☐	☐	_____
Short 'i' words	☐	☐	_____
Long 'i' words	☐	☐	_____
Short 'o' words	☐	☐	_____
Long 'o' words	☐	☐	_____
Short 'u' words	☐	☐	_____
Long 'u' words	☐	☐	_____
Negative prefixes	☐	☐	_____
'pre' and 're'	☐	☐	_____
Adding prefixes	☐	☐	_____
'al'	☐	☐	_____

Spelling rule	Addressed		Comments
	Yes	No	
Greek prefixes	☐	☐	_____
Latin prefixes	☐	☐	_____
'ed' and 'ing'	☐	☐	_____
Adding suffixes to 'e' words	☐	☐	_____
Adding suffixes to 'y' words	☐	☐	_____
'y'	☐	☐	_____
'ly'	☐	☐	_____
'ful'	☐	☐	_____
Comparatives	☐	☐	_____
Greek suffixes	☐	☐	_____
Latin suffixes	☐	☐	_____
Choosing suffix endings	☐	☐	_____
'ible' and 'able'	☐	☐	_____
'al' and 'ic'	☐	☐	_____
'ary'	☐	☐	_____
'ive'	☐	☐	_____
'tion' and 'sion'	☐	☐	_____
Plurals – words that end in 'ch', 'sh', 's', 'x' and 'z'	☐	☐	_____
Plurals – words that end in 'y'	☐	☐	_____
Plurals – words that end in 'f' and 'fe'	☐	☐	_____
Plurals – words that end in 'o'	☐	☐	_____
Special forms of plurals	☐	☐	_____
Homophones	☐	☐	_____
Similar words	☐	☐	_____
Difficult words	☐	☐	_____

LOOK, SAY, COVER	WRITE	CHECK
	_____	_____
	_____	_____
	_____	_____
	_____	_____

LOOK, SAY, COVER	WRITE	CHECK
	_____	_____
	_____	_____
	_____	_____
	_____	_____

LOOK, SAY, COVER	WRITE	CHECK
	_____	_____
	_____	_____
	_____	_____
	_____	_____

LOOK, SAY, COVER	WRITE	CHECK
	_____	_____
	_____	_____
	_____	_____
	_____	_____

LOOK, SAY, COVER	WRITE	CHECK
	_____	_____
	_____	_____
	_____	_____
	_____	_____

LOOK, SAY, COVER	WRITE	CHECK
	_____	_____
	_____	_____
	_____	_____
	_____	_____